Praise for B<

"*Be Safe Not Sorry* is the manual for personal safety. David Fowler tackles the subject of violent crime by offering core principles and commonsense advice which empowers, rather than frightens."

— David Cole, Corporate Security Trainer

"*Be Safe Not Sorry* is a book every family should have at home. It's required reading for every parent who wants to keep his or her child safe from the dangers of the real world."

— Dr. Steve Albrecht, PHR, CPP, retired San Diego Police Department, author of *Ticking Bombs: Defusing Violence in the Workplace and Tactical Perfection for Street Cops.*

"With over 20 years in the Security and Law Enforcement profession, you would think I would just about know it all. I was wrong. *Be Safe Not Sorry* is a great book. It's truly worth its weight in gold."

— J C Shah, Risk Manager, Phoenix Protective Corporation

"This book may save your life. If you're looking for *the* book on this important topic, this is it!"

— David Behar, Security and Emergency Management, Snohomish County Public Utility District

"Anyone that has ever had a second thought and concern about crime and violence should read this book."

— Ed Mumphrey, Seattle Mariners Corporate Security, Seattle, WA

"*Be Safe Not Sorry* wakes the mind up to see life as it truly is and to take notice and stock of our surroundings. Stop and smell the roses without getting stung by the bee in the flower."

— Sean Stoddard, Training Specialist, Viejas Casino, Alpine, CA

"I've had the privilege to attend Dave's training classes, and each time I learn something new. After reading his book, I would place it on the 'must read list'... Dave's book is another valuable tool in personnel safety and awareness."

— Lieutenant Robert Murray, Maricopa County Animal Control Enforcement Division

"David Fowler's book is a must read for anyone... offering readers skills to protect themselves and others from becoming unwilling victims of crime and violence."

— Dean O'Loughlin, Personal Safety Solutions, Australia

"*Be Safe Not Sorry* is a straight forward common sense approach to personal safety. A must read for the general public as well as security professionals."

— Scott A. Hemingway, Director of Healthcare Security, APG Security

"Dave Fowler has created concepts and specific interventions that are easy to understand, internalize and make a part of everyone's daily life. His style is easy and flows as if he is speaking directly to each of us. While the concepts of self-defense and awareness are not new, we now have a fresh approach."

— Mark Mooring, LAPD Sergeant and Chief of Protective Services, Santa Clara County, Retired

"*Be Safe Not Sorry* was great! Even my 16-year-old niece read the book."

— Jennifer Yazzie, Security Supervisor, Fort Defiance Indian Hospital

"*Be Safe Not Sorry* is an awesome book. Thank you for giving me more tools and options to keep myself and the important people in my life SAFER. I will continue to read and re-read it often."

— Jo Jauregui, Human Resources Professional, NorthBay Healthcare

BE SAFE
NOT SORRY

---

the art and science of keeping YOU and your family SAFE from crime and violence

Victor!
Be Safe
+
Good Bless!

DAVID FOWLER

This book includes information from many sources and gathered from many personal experiences. It is published for general reference and is not intended to be a substitute for independent verification by readers when necessary and appropriate. The book is sold with the understanding that the neither the author nor publisher is engaged in rendering any legal, medical, tactical, technical or psychological advice. The publisher and author disclaim any personal liability, directly or indirectly, for advice or information presented within. Although the author and publisher have prepared this manuscript with utmost care and diligence and have made every effort to ensure the accuracy and completeness of the information contained within, we assume no responsibility for errors, inaccuracies, omissions or inconsistencies.

Publisher's Cataloging-in-Publication
Fowler, David

Fowler, David
Be Safe Not Sorry: the art and science of keeping you and your family safe from crime and violence/David Fowler

– 2nd ed.2013
Includes index.

ISBN: 978-0-9826163-0-7

Library of Congress Control Number: 2010911902

ATTN: QUANTITY DISCOUNTS ARE AVAILABLE TO YOUR COMPANY, EDUCATIONAL INSTITUTION OR WRITING ORGANIZATION for reselling, educational purposes, subscription incentives, gifts, or fundraising campaigns. For more information, please contact the publisher at Personal Safety Training Inc., P.O. Box 2957, Coeur d' Alene, ID 83816 (208)664-5551 dave@personalsafetytraining.com

To my father, Gary W. Fowler

Your memory inspires me to share my message

■   ■   ■

Disclaimer

Neither the author nor the publisher, Personal Safety Training, Inc., do not dictate policies or procedures for the use of any self-defense or any physical intervention authorized for use by a department/agency or private individual. The suggestions/options disseminated in this book are simply that, suggestions or options. Each individual, department or agency is responsible for developing their own "policies and procedures" regarding the use of self-defense and physical intervention for their personnel and for themselves.

Although every effort has been made for this book to be complete and accurate, it is impossible to predict, discuss or plan for every circumstance or situation which might arise in the course of defending yourself and any contact with a violent or aggressive person(s) or during a crime. Every reader must always take into consideration their experience, physical abilities, professional responsibilities, agency and department procedures and state, local and federal legal requirements. With this in mind, each reader must evaluate the recommendations and techniques contained in this book and decide for himself (herself) which should be used and under what circumstances. Each reader assumes risk of loss, injury, and damages associated with this book and use of the information obtained in it. The author and publisher, Personal Safety Training, Inc. cannot guarantee or warrant the legal, medical, tactical or technical suggestions/options in this book. Any implied warranties are expressly disavowed.

Certain names, dates, places and circumstances have been altered and or changed to protect the identity of the individuals involved. Any similarity to any and all other persons is purely coincidental.

Acknowledgements

First and foremost I would like to thank God.

I would also like to thank the many teachers, instructors, mentors and friends who have helped make this book a reality. Without your help, inspiration and invaluable knowledge this wouldn't have been possible. To all of you, I am eternally grateful.

I would also like to thank the thousands of individuals whom I have worked with, whose direct and indirect contributions to this book have made it possible for me to do what I feel on purpose to do.

Special thanks to the following individuals for their support and technical advice: Mark Costello, Brian Goodwin, Doug Kearns, Brian Keltz, Mark Loudin, Mark Mooring, Steve Pettillo, Patrick Seifert, and C. R. Your martial wisdom and inspiration echoes through these pages.

Very special thanks to my editor, Theresa Renner. Without your help and patience this book wouldn't have happened. Your grace and wordsmithing expertise has allowed me to influence and help others. We both have no idea how truly amazing this really is. I know this is just the beginning.

I would also like to thank my family for their support through this process; My mom, Nancy, daughters Kaley and Jacquelyn, sisters Carol and Julie, grandparents, aunts, uncles and cousins. I love you all so much!

And finally, a most heartfelt thanks to my wife, Genelle Fowler. Your commitment, grace, honor, kindness, gentleness and most all, Love, has made all of this possible. ILYWAMH.

Contents

Preface

I was a victim of a violent crime.

When I tell people that, they are taken aback. I'm six feet tall, I have competed as a black belt in Karate, I was a professional full-contact fighter, and I've done the Ironman Triathlon three times. But a lot of that is *because* I was a victim.

I became a victim one morning when I was twelve years old. I got to the bus stop about half an hour early that day, as I usually did. There were three other kids my age who took the bus from that stop, and we liked to throw the ball around before school. At twelve years old, we had a lot of energy to burn up.

As we goofed off and threw the football around, a car pulled up to us. The four teenage boys inside—all of them probably somewhere between seventeen and nineteen years old—started harassing us verbally, shouting insults and offensive remarks. At first, I just thought it was strange. Why were a bunch of older guys, who we didn't know, interested in us at all? Then, apparently, they decided shouting insults wasn't enough fun, so they got out of their car. As they all climbed out, we could see beer cans rolling around on the floorboards.

Obviously, at that point in my life, I had no idea how to handle aggressive behavior. I didn't know how to deal with four big drunk guys. None of us did. When they started getting physical, pushing us around, the smart thing would have been to run. Instead, I smarted off to them.

That was a mistake.

From that point on, I was the focus of their rage. I don't remember the beating itself very well. I know my friends were too scared to do anything but watch. I remember that no cars drove by. No one tried to help me.

Eventually, they got bored with beating me and left. I got up and dusted myself off, not making eye contact with the other boys. When the bus got there, I got on, acting as normal as I could. I hurt, but I could tell I didn't need to go to the hospital. I just sat there on the bus, trying to ignore the stares.

I quickly discovered that the worst part wasn't over. The busted lip, the black eye, the cuts, the scrapes would heal. But as soon as I got to school, the teachers and other students started asking, "David, what happened? Are you ok?" Somehow, that made it worse. If we could have all pretended that my face wasn't swelling and bruised, that I wasn't scraped and bleeding, it might have been different. But I now discovered a new feeling: humiliation.

Nobody can explain to a twelve-year-old boy that it wasn't his fault that a bunch of drunk young men beat him up. Of course there was no way I could have defended myself against that. But that didn't matter. It was still utterly humiliating. For days, I had to walk around with the evidence of my weakness all over my face.

The worst times were at night. I would lay in bed, trying to go to sleep, but instead reliving the beating, over and over again. Reliving the pain. Reliving the helplessness. Reliving the fear. This was the late 1970s, and the only people who knew about "post-traumatic stress disorder" (PTSD) were mental health professionals. It wasn't commonly understood yet. It didn't occur to my parents, and it certainly didn't occur to me, that PTSD was the name for what I was experiencing. I just knew I was angry, and I felt helpless.

After a few weeks of spending my nights like this, I reached a decision: No one was ever going to hurt me like that again. Ever.

At twelve years old, the solutions to problems are straight-forward. I didn't ever want to be beaten up again, therefore I needed to learn how to fight. Simple solution. If I became a good fighter, better than anyone who might try to take me on, I would never be humiliated again. I would be in charge of any difficult, dangerous situation that I found myself in.

Through a neighbor, I knew someone who was a black belt and an instructor at a local Karate school. Karate seemed like the best way to learn to fight. I knew that anyone who studied Karate didn't get hassled. And I wanted to be someone who didn't get hassled. When I told my parents I wanted to study Karate, they quickly agreed. My mother, in particular, didn't like the idea of fighting at all, but she and my father knew I would also learn a lot of other, more important things in Karate—things like discipline, self-respect, respect for others, compassion, and dignity.

By the age of eighteen, I was competing as a black belt. I'd competed in Karate tournaments throughout my teenage years using *kata* (which are choreographed movements), and semi-contact sparring. But that was all controlled. At the age of eighteen, I was ready for a new challenge. I wanted to test my fighting skills to see how good I really was—and I wanted to see how effective my skills were in an actual fight.

At that time, the best way to test my fighting skills was by competing in full contact Karate (these days, it's called kickboxing, or ultimate fighting). Almost immediately, I realized something important: I was really, really good at fighting. For more than ten years, I fought in bout after bout, improving my fighting skills each time. In all those years I competed, I only lost twice. I had achieved the goal I had set for myself when I was twelve years old: no one would ever be able to attack me and get the better of me again.

In 1996, I was getting ready to fight for the Super Middleweight Championship of the World in Vancouver, British Columbia, Canada. I was happily married by then, had two fantastic kids, and a job I enjoyed, working in the security department of a large medical center, where I had started as a security officer and worked my way up to management. I was on top of the world.

Two months prior to my title fight, I had another life-altering experience, the thing that would change the direction of my life even more powerfully than that beating that had changed my life at age twelve.

I was at work one day at the medical center when one of my father's coworkers came through the doors of the emergency department. I happened to be in the emergency department security office when he came in, so it was just a stroke of luck that I was right there to greet him. My dad's office was thirty-five miles away, so I knew he wasn't just dropping by. I figured he was there for medical treatment.

"Hey, Ron," I said as I walked up to him and held out my hand. "What are you doing over here? Do you need to see a doc?"

No," he said. "Dave, I just really need to talk to you," he seemed distracted and anxious.

"Oh," I was a little taken aback. "Uh, sure. What's up?" I asked, confused.

"No, I *really* need to talk to you," he said, glancing around the emergency department lobby where we were standing. "Is there somewhere we can go to talk privately?"

"Sure, Ron, let's go to the security office." He followed me down the hall to my office, and we sat down, facing each other. Then he reached over and took my hands. Now I was *really* confused.

"Dave, I have some really bad news," he took a breath. "We lost your dad today."

At first, what he said just didn't compute.

"What? What do you mean?" I asked. Now I could see how distraught he was.

"Dave, we lost your dad today. He passed away at work."

I sat there, stunned. It was the punch I hadn't seen coming. My father had suffered a massive heart attack. At the age of fifty-two, my father was dead.

Like a lot of people in that situation, faced with the sudden gaping hole in my world where my father had been, it forced me to do some reflection on my own life. With an unflinching look at myself, my priorities, and the direction of my life, I came to the unpleasant realization that I was all about one person: I was all about Dave.

Suddenly, that wasn't good enough anymore. I wanted to find a way to take the skills, the talents, and the knowledge I had and help other people. I wanted a way to give back.

I dropped out of that championship bout. I never got in the full-contact ring again.

I had started out on my life's path as a twelve-year-old kid who didn't want to be pushed around. I had based my whole life on making myself safe. Now I looked at everything I knew, everything I was using to train my employees at the medical center, and I realized I was training them in something far more important than how to fight: I was training them how *not* to fight. Their job, and mine, was dealing with aggressive, even dangerous people (who are present in hospitals and medical centers more often than you would think) and defusing and de-escalating situations so that everyone got out of them safely.

I asked myself the question, how could I give back? How could I impart the lessons I had learned to other people? I had twenty-one guys working under me at the medical center, so I had a captive audience to start teaching the things I had learned over the years on the street and in the *dojo*. I researched and attended training programs, I read books on psychology, behavior, martial arts, self-improvement, communication—anything that would help me teach people how to be safe.

I began giving training seminars to the security departments at other medical centers. Over the course of several years, I expanded and improved my courses. I adapted my seminars to be taught to personnel in the security industry, schools and education centers, corporations, behavioral health centers, even firefighters, law enforcement officers and military personnel. Eventually, I became so booked with my training seminars that I had to quit my "day job" at the medical center.

A few years ago, I realized that there was one huge segment of the population

I was missing, a large group of people who really needed this information, but that wasn't targeted in any of my seminars: the average citizen. *You*. I didn't have a specific training course for everyday living. But I had the knowledge and techniques I use every day to keep myself and my family safe. And I knew it was time to put them together to get the word out to people. You don't need pepper spray, a black belt, or even a gun. You need knowledge.

I have worked in the protection and security industry for more than twenty years. For several years, I have been toying with the idea of putting everything I have learned together into a "personal safety handbook." Then in 2005, something happened that made me realize I *had* to put this book together—that I owe it to everyone out there who has not been fortunate enough to learn the things I have learned. It was one of those things that "hit so close to home," it shook me up, my friends, and my entire community.

In May 2005, convicted child molester Joseph Edward Duncan, III, entered a home less than twenty miles from my own. The account we have comes from the only survivor of the family, seven-year-old, Shasta Groene. Holding the adults with a twelve-gauge shotgun, Duncan bound the mother,

her boyfriend, and thirteen-year-old Shane Groene. Duncan had two objectives: he wanted Shasta and her nine-year-old brother, Dylan. Duncan murdered the mother, her boyfriend and Shane. Then he took Shasta and Dylan, and headed toward Montana.

An Amber Alert was issued for Shasta and Dylan. Police interviewed and investigated everyone close to the family. They had absolutely no evidence leading them to Duncan, because his only connection to this family was that he had been watching them in the days leading up to the murder and abduction.

Around two in the morning on July 2, 2005, Duncan reappeared in Shasta's hometown, Coeur d'Alene, Idaho—with Shasta—at a Denny's restaurant. By this time, photos of Shasta and Dylan were on billboards all over the area. Their faces were on the news every night. Nationwide Amber Alerts kept them in the public consciousness. The people in Denny's quickly recognized Shasta, called police, and kept Duncan and Shasta from leaving until police could get there. Within hours, Shasta was reunited with her father, safe at last.

Dylan's body was later found in a shallow grave in Montana. Duncan had kept both Shasta and Dylan for almost two months, molesting and abusing them before he murdered Dylan. It was a miracle Shasta was rescued.

Of course, the Groene case terrified all of us, not just those of us who live in this sleepy little corner of northern Idaho, but the whole nation. What kind of monsters are out there these days? How can we possibly protect ourselves against an armed madman who breaks into our home to steal our children?

I wasn't the only person who lost sleep over this case. But I was asking myself different questions. What if the Groene family had had access to the information I have had access to? What if they had a plan for an armed intruder? What if they had known to never, ever let anyone tie you up and control you with fear? What about all the other things I have learned over the years? Could they have survived? Would the news reports have read, "Armed Intruder Driven Out of Home" instead of "Three Found Murdered, Two Children Missing"? And the question that kept coming back to me, over and over again: How can I get this information out to people? I realized it was time to put together what I have learned, so I can teach other people how tokeep themselves and their families safe.

Of course, I am not saying, I *cannot* say, that if the Groene Family had known these things, then that awful tragedy, with little Shasta as the last survivor, would not have happened. No one can say that. "If only" is a pointless game to play. But by using the tools I lay out in this book, you will have a much better chance of coming out of any dangerous situation alive. Maybe not uninjured, maybe not without some scars, emotional or physical, but alive.

So here it is. A simple handbook for everyday personal safety. Concepts to incorporate into your life that will empower you in any aggressive or dangerous situation. Things to think about. Things to teach your children. Ways to keep you and your family safe.

Introduction

You see it every time you turn on the TV, use the internet, or pick up a magazine or newspaper: Crime. Assault. Robbery. Rape. Murder. Many of us have the same reaction, "That's awful! But that would never happen to *me*."

Are you sure? Most of those victims probably felt the same way. At twelve years old, I certainly didn't think I would be a victim. So what happened?

Crime reports verify one thing: people with the right skills stand an excellent chance of avoiding or surviving a crime. That's what you'll learn from this book: how to avoid becoming a victim of a violent crime, and how to survive if you are one.

Here in the United States, the FBI has something called the "crime clock," a statistical compilation where they track crime. Every second, every minute and every hour of every single day, crimes are being committed. According to the most recent statistics:

- Every 4.8 seconds, a theft is committed
- Every 14.5 seconds, a burglary is committed (breaking into a house)
- Every 28.8 seconds, a vehicle is stolen
- Every 36.8 seconds, a person is assaulted
- Every 5.8 minutes, a person is raped
- Every 1.2 minutes, a robbery takes place (robbery is the use of force against a person to steal from them)
- Every 31 minutes, someone is murdered

What about you? Have you ever been in a situation that didn't feel safe?

Have you ever been verbally assaulted—somebody in your face, calling you names, verbally harassing you... even threatening you? Have you ever been physically assaulted, or witnessed an assault? What about your belongings and your environment? Have you ever felt that they were at risk? Do you know someone who has been a victim of crime and violence?

This book is about prevention and intervention—learning proactive responses to deal with crime and violence.

"Proactive" is a word that gets thrown around a lot these days, but what does it really mean? For our purposes, proactive individuals recognize the importance of responsibility. They don't blame circumstances or conditions for their behavior or their outcomes. Their behavior is a product of their own conscious choices based on values rather than circumstances. Reactive individuals, on the other hand, are often affected by their physical and social environment; they're driven by their feelings, circumstances and conditions. Socially, reactive individuals feel good when people treat them well. But when people don't, they can become defensive or aggressive.

In every incident in our lives, whether it involves a threatening situation, a crime or a violent situation, you are part of the equation. Therefore, your response will determine the outcome of the situation. It's the I+R=O equation[1], Incident plus Response equals Outcome.

We've all heard the old saying, "Life is not about what happens to us. It's about how we choose to respond to what happens to us." Life is ten percent what happens to us and ninety percent how we respond to it. By taking responsibility for our personal safety, we can make conscious, informed choices about our environments, the people around us and the places we frequent.

Whose responsibility is your personal safety? YOURS. And the first step is reading this book.

---

[1] I first heard of this from Jack Canfield, one of the co-creators of the *Chicken Soup for the Soul* books. He used "event + response = outcome." I've modified it to "incident + response = outcome," because, for the purpose of this book, we'll be talking about violent or potentially violent incidents.

Empowerment, NOT Fear

Fear limits your productivity, your ability to live a safe, harmonious, successful life. I know that in my life I want to be safer so I can live a harmonious life and be the person I want to be. This book is about not letting fear rule you. It's not about looking for the violent criminal around every corner. It's about learning the kind of mindset that will keep you safe. And it's about creating habits, and learning practices and behaviors that become so second nature, you don't even think about them. You'll learn to keep yourself and your loved ones safe, without stopping your life or instilling fear in anyone.

AVADE®

Back in 2001, I developed a personal safety training program called AVADE®. The program is for everyone, not just the industries that I normally train people in; in fact, I taught the first classes to American Red Cross personnel at local chapters. In this book, you will learn everything people learn in my training seminars. AVADE® stands for:

Awareness
Vigilance
Avoidance
Defense
Escape

AVADE® training is based on my conscious study and research. After thirty years studying and working in the fields of safety, security, self-defense, and martial arts, I've done my homework. The comprehensive bibliography in the back of the book will show you what this material is based on, aside from my personal experience: proven psychology of criminals and victims; the physiology of aggressive behavior; psychology of success; and other mind-related sciences. With AVADE®, you'll learn how to:

• Increase your awareness in all areas of your life

• Increase your overall safety in every area of your life

- Increase your confidence
- Increase your quality of life
- Increase your self-improvement
- Feel more empowered
- Increase your sense of overall peace
- Increase your ability to protect yourself and others
- Reduce fear
- Reduce stress in every aspect of your life
- Reduce potential for injury
- Reduce liability risk by learning what is lawful and what is not lawful
- Reduce loss of personal property
- Reduce feelings of inadequacy and inability to respond to situations.
- Increase your ability to respond to dangerous situations

The AVADE® philosophy goes beyond the typical quick-fix self-defense and personal safety training programs. AVADE® will teach you how to live a safe, positive, balanced life with the habits, skills and actions you need to stay safe. You'll learn to take proactive, preventative measures to defend yourself and others, use lawful defensive intervention, and how to have an awareness of all your environments—home, school, work, your car, your neighborhood, the parking lot of the store you're shopping in. AVADE® will teach you to be safe wherever you are—not paranoid, not scared, but empowered and powerful in ways that act as repellent to predators.

"Every human has four endowments—self-awareness, conscience, independent will, and creative imagination. These give us the ultimate human freedom...the power to choose, to respond, to change."

- Stephen R. Covey, *The 7 Habits of Highly Effective People*

Chapter 1

Awareness

Awareness will keep you safe. It will keep you alive. Your awareness is the most important prevention measure when it comes to dangerous and threatening situations.

Awareness is a mental state or ability to perceive, feel, or be conscious of people, emotions, conditions, events, objects, and patterns. The key to awareness is knowledge and understanding. We've been taught to be aware since we were little kids. Remember your parents telling you to stop and look both ways before you crossed the street? Then, when you were old enough to drive, your driver's ed teachers and your parents drummed into you to be aware and alert, to pay attention when you're behind the wheel, because that vehicle you're in can be very dangerous. You could hurt yourself, or you could hurt someone else. That's why you check your mirrors, you look around, you make sure that no one is in that lane that you turn into. Eventually, that awareness becomes a habit. You use that awareness to keep yourself and others safe.

Military personnel are taught what is called "situational awareness." Soldiers in the field need to be aware of what is going on around them to keep them safe. Their senses are heightened to see enemy soldiers, to listen for different sounds that might let them know that their enemy is advancing—footsteps, helicopter noise, airplanes, incoming artillery, whatever it may be. If you're walking alone through a parking structure at night (which you should avoid doing), your senses will be heightened to hear any sound that might alert you that danger is present. In a parking structure, someone breathing right behind you may equal danger; in a crowded elevator, it probably doesn't mean anything. It all depends on the situation.

How Aware Are You?

When you change your awareness, you change your life. Your awareness affects everything you do, both personally and professionally. There are many levels of awareness in day-to-day life that are important to understand:

Conscious Awareness. The awareness that you're using right now; that is, your ability to focus and consciously perceive and feel what is being said or happening at this moment of time. This is your ability to recognize and process what's going on around you right now. Who's in your house? Your office? Is someone suspicious parked near your car? Are those raised voices on the street you're walking on just excited, or are they threatening?

Self-Awareness. Your ability to recognize and understand your mental and physical abilities and your limitations. Self-awareness is knowing what you can and you can't do, what your mental limits are and what your physical limits are. If I asked you to go out and run a marathon right now, with your current self-awareness, you might say, "Uh, no, I'm not able to do that." But if you had to run out of a burning building, carrying your fifty-pound child, you almost certainly *could* do that. If I asked you to translate this paragraph into ancient Latin, you might look at that and go, "You know I just can't do that." But if you needed to find the closest exit in an airplane in the dark, you can do that. That is also self-awareness, what you can't do and what you can do. Are you aware of what's going on inside of you right now? Are you anxious or fuzzy-headed from hunger? Antsy from caffeine? Sluggish from too little sleep? Are you aware of how you're feeling? Irritated from frustration? Happy over some good news? Distracted? How does your self-awareness of what's going on with you right now affect your ability to keep yourself safe? You'll learn how in the pages to come.

Emotional Awareness. Your ability to recognize and feel the emotions and feelings of others, as well as your own. Are you aware of how the people around you—or people whom you may encounter—are feeling? That unsettling co-worker—did his wife finally leave him? Is he angry? Morose? Your spouse is quiet—because of a bad day? Or something he or she won't talk about? Emotional awareness tunes you in to other people's feelings.

Non-conscious Awareness. The state of awareness where situational awareness, self-awareness, conscious awareness, and emotional awareness have become habitual. We should all try to achieve this level. It's the awareness level where you keep yourself and your loved ones safe. It's the level where personal safety habits are so ingrained, you don't even think about them. They're as natural as breathing. (We'll talk more about habits a little later on.)

Higher Awareness. The highest state of awareness, encompassing all the other levels of awarenesses that we have just talked about, as well as your Spiritual Awareness. (In the final chapter, we will explore the spiritual side of personal safety.)

Achieving Habitual Awareness

You've heard the term, "the tip of the iceberg," right? Psychologists like to use icebergs as an analogy for the human mind. That tip, the part you can see, sticks out of the water and accounts for about 10% of the mass of the iceberg. That part represents the "conscious mind," the part of the mind that you're using right now; it's where you think. The mass of the iceberg that lies below the ocean represents the non-conscious mind, which is also called the subconscious mind. The non-conscious mind runs the body, it allows us to breathe, digest food, etc. I like to take this analogy one point further: the iceberg is floating in the ocean, and I liken that ocean to "the universal mind." The universal mind is our connectedness to everything, to all things.

Understanding these three categories of the human mind—conscious, non-conscious, and universal—will give you a higher understanding of why your amazing mind is the most important part of your safety and ability to protect yourself.

Constant communication is going on between these three categories of the mind. The conscious mind communicates with the non-conscious mind, the non-conscious mind communicates to the universal mind, and backwards, the universal mind connects to the non-conscious mind, the non-conscious mind connects to the conscious mind; there is no separation, there is no order. But you can train your non-conscious mind, and you can train your conscious mind.

Good Habits, Bad Habits, Safe Habits

Creatures of habit. That's what we are. Habits are acquired patterns of behavior that occur automatically without us thinking about them. These are things that we repeatedly do over and over. Habits can be good or bad. We do the same thing every day without conscious thought. We don't think about it; we just do it. The way we answer the phone, the way we greet people, how we shake hands, the way we gesture, smile or not smile are all our habits as well. Habits are ingrained in us. They're stamped into our non-conscious mind, for better or worse. But you can have control over what is stamped in your mind.

What are some of your personal safety habits? When you get in your car, you probably start your car, fasten your seatbelt, maybe you adjust your mirrors. When you get home at night, you have your keys ready, then you lock your door right behind you once you're inside. Those are examples of personal safety habits, things you have trained your non-conscious brain to do automatically, without thinking about it. My goal in this book is to increase the number of, and effectiveness of, your personal safety habits.

For example, before you even fasten your seatbelt, you should lock your car doors. Did you notice that omission? I left it out to see if you would. Maybe you just thought, "Hmmm. There's something wrong with that sequence of events." Maybe you didn't notice anything at all. I want to raise your awareness, so that you're aware and safe. Make it a new habit: *when you get in your car, lock the doors right away.*

After taking my class, a 38-year-old woman, Erin told me this story:

> I work out at a 24-hour, key-in gym. It's women on-
> ly, and we have great security there. I had been going

during regular hours, but my schedule changed, and I started going late at night, when there is absolutely no one around—not in the gym, not in that area of town. No one. I always parked in the same spot. One night, I came out of the gym and realized that my regular spot is right next to a large shrub, by the driver's door. Someone could hide behind that bush, and I'd be almost *in* my car before I'd notice them. I never paid attention during the busy day, but I stopped parking in that spot—even during the day.

Her *awareness* had changed. Also, note that she hadn't become terrified into not going out and doing the things she wanted to do. She was just a lot more aware of her surroundings. That's the kind of safety habit you'll learn in this book. You'll break bad habits, and you'll develop good ones, by increasing your awareness.[2]

Creating new habits takes action. It takes commitment and it takes your ability to identify what you want to create as a habit. Anyone can create new personal safety and self-defense habits. One of the ways to do this is by playing what I call the "21 Game"—it's the process of making small adjustments in your behavior, for twenty-one days straight. Twenty-one days of repeatedly doing what we intend to do to create a new habit or change, or eliminate, an old habit. (This rule obviously would not be applicable to a limiting habit that you've had for an extended time. Long-term habits have roots like trees that run very deep. Changing or eliminating long-term habits could take a year or more.)

If you're going to create a new habit, or identify and eliminate an old habit, you've got to make a clear decision in your conscious mind. Then, through repetition, you change your *non-conscious* mind. Having a clear and defined personal safety goal is a first powerful step in creating a new habit. You can take action on your new habit by the process of visualization, which will train your non-conscious mind. When you visualize, you add repetition, and we all know that repetition is the first law of learning. We repeat to remember.

---

[2] I want to be clear that I am talking about being *aware*, not being *paranoid*. It the next chapter, we'll go into more detail about "hyper-vigilance," which is counter-productive and causes anxiety.

Remember Erin, who knew she should change her parking space? I asked her how long it took her to make that a habit. She laughed and told me:

> This is embarrassing to admit, but it took a while. Every night I'd pull into that parking lot, with a million other things on my mind. I think two or three more times, I parked in that same spot and went in. I'd come out of the gym and see that shrub and think, "Erin! What are you doing?" So I got in the car that night and said, *out loud*, "Next time, I will park over there," and I'd point to the spot I knew was a safer bet. I said that—and even pointed—three times that night! The next night, I *still* pulled into the wrong spot! But before I even turned my car off, I remembered and I pulled out and parked in the other space I had designated. It was like muscle memory. I *always* pulled into that same spot! It definitely took a while before I automatically parked in the "right" spot.

The conscious mind is very powerful. Erin used it to program her non-conscious mind, then she used repetition to make it a habit.

Your conscious mind thinks, reasons, allows you to choose and exercise free will. It gives you the ability to evaluate, choose options, make decisions, and to communicate with your body through the sensations of sight, sound, smell, taste, and touch. Through your conscious mind, you can judge. You can judge these words you're reading—are they truthful? Do you understand them? You have the ability to judge and make decisions with your conscious mind. You can evaluate situations, circumstances, and understanding with the conscious mind. Your ability to remember is part of the conscious mind, especially the short-term memory.

Our non-conscious mind is where our instinct lies. Instinctually, we respond in certain ways. Humans—along with a lot of other animals—have what is called a startle effect. If you're scared or surprised or startled, your eyes will get really big, your hands come up to protect yourself, you step back. Usually, you end up laughing about it. Usually, it's nothing more than a dog barking in a car as you walk past it, or a person coming around a corner while you're deep in thought. In our conscious mind, we talk ourselves down off the ledge of the adrenaline rush of being startled.

We're so used to relying on our conscious mind, when something interrupts our rational thought, we find it hard to act on it. The universal mind does not seem particularly rational. It communicates to the non-conscious mind in ways that let our body know that something just isn't right. It's as though it bypasses your conscious mind altogether.

Have you ever had that feeling when the hair on the back of your neck stands up? That's the universal mind saying, "Hey, something isn't right here." The non-conscious mind receives the message, and sends signals to the body saying, "OK, get goose bumps. Make the hair on the back of my neck stand up." Heart rate increases, adrenalin and cortisol production goes up, all the things that signal "Danger!"

Then your conscious mind perceives these physiological changes, and you reject it, or judge it worthy of concern. We make a decision that we're overreacting to some perceived threat, or we decide, "OK, I need to do something about this. I need to get out of there. I need to run. I need to flee. I need to do *something*." There is no separation: conscious, non-conscious, universal mind. The understanding of these three categories of the mind is essential in your ability to increase your awareness, to understand the programming of the non-conscious mind, and understand how those signals are received in your conscious mind.[3]

The last category of the human mind is the universal mind. We will explore this part of the mind later on when we discuss the topic of intuition because intuition is part of this connectiveness and the universal mind.

Create Your Safety

So the universal mind and the non-conscious mind are tuned in to protect us at all times. Now you need to train your conscious mind to be tuned in to that, too. And it's a lot easier than you think, because *the conscious mind is where you create.*

Visualization has gotten a lot of press in the last twenty years or so. Athletes routinely use it to improve their games. Michael Jordan, arguably

---

[3] We'll talk more about accepting or rejecting those danger signals, and the use of our intuition, in Chapter 2.

the best basketball player ever, used it before every game. In his book *For the Love of the Game*, Michael talks about sitting in the locker room going over the events of the game in his mind's eye prior to walking out onto the court. Sure, he had a lot of natural talent, and he worked his butt off, being the first on, and the last one off, the practice court. But, before every game, he also took time to visualize his performance the way he wanted it to be. When I was a full-contact fighter, I did this before every bout—except two. And those were the only two I ever lost.

In the 1980s, sports psychologist Dennis Waitley introduced visualization into the training programs for U.S. Olympic athletes. In the movie *The Secret,* Waitley shares his insight into visual motor rehearsal, a process of using the mind and visualization. When they hooked the athletes up to biofeedback machines, they discovered something truly astounding: when they had the athletes run through their event in their minds, *the same muscles fired as when the athlete physically performed their sport.*

It's a simple, powerful tool that you can use. If Erin, the woman who changed her parking habit, had *visualized* parking in the correct spot, it would have taken her less time to make that a new habit. Use your conscious mind to train your non-conscious mind to protect yourself. Have you ever prepared for a job interview? Maybe even practiced for them by having a friend or teacher "interview" you? It's the same concept. It helps you think through all possible scenarios of your event, and gives you the chance to envision the best outcome. If this feels too weird, here's an easy way to start:

Stage 1: Create the scene in your mind's eye of the event, incident or situation you want to create—or re-create. If you had an incident that went badly, you can re-create it to make it go the way you wished it had gone. I did that with my life-changing incident when I was a twelve-year-old. I envisioned myself coming out on top of that exchange. We're going to imagine a scene that could happen to anyone at work.

Imagine you're at your workplace, sitting at your desk, and you're busy working on a report. Suddenly, you hear a loud commotion, shouting, from down the hall. You get up from your work area and you start to approach the area the shouting is coming from. As you get closer, you realize it's the reception area.

Stage 2: Make the scene as clear and colorful as possible. Focus your mind's eye as you create your clear, concise mental scene. Imagine exactly how the reception area in your office looks. Imagine the receptionist you know sitting at her desk, with her latte sitting right next to her phone—whatever little details make it real to you. Imagine the color of your office walls, the coffee scent of the latte. Now imagine that a very aggressive individual is posturing over the receptionist and her work area. She's scooted her chair away from the desk area, she is visibly scared, she's leaning back, her eyes are wide open, she's frightened of this aggressive individual who is towering over her, yelling at her, using obscenities and expletives about how unhappy he is.

Stage 3: "Lights, Focus, Camera and Action!" Now that the scene is clear and focused, give it action. As the director of your mental movie you direct everything in it. What you do, what other people do, all the events of your mental movie. So, now imagine how you approach this situation, how far you stand away from this aggressive individual. Visualize your body language, making—or not making—eye contact. Imagine what you say to this aggressive individual and how you say it. Imagine how this individual responds to you. This is your movie, so now imagine this individual's response to you: his posture becomes less aggressive; his tone is less threatening; his voice is not as loud. In your mind, you are de-escalating this situation, you are managing this aggressive behavior. Imagine what you say, imagine what you do, imagine what the individual does.

Stage 4: The plot/outcome is up to you! You decide what happens, when it happens and who it happens to. You are the hero of your mental movie. You never lose in your mind's eye when you create, direct and choreograph the mental movie. You always win. You always prevail. You always escape. You always use the appropriate defensive intervention.

Now see in your mind's eye escorting this individual to the exit doors of your building. See him thank you for your appropriateness and your professional manner with how you've handled this situation.

Stage 5: Feel what it is like to be the star of your mental movie. How does that feel to you when you win, when you survive, when you escape, when you avoid the situation? So when a stressful event happens, the mind goes back automatically to that memory store bank and retrieves that information, so you respond in the appropriate way.

Now see in your mind's eye walking back to the receptionist. She is so happy as she gets up and runs towards you, and thanks you for how you responded, how you saved her in this situation. See in your mind's eye how you respond to her, letting her know that it was your pleasure to be there to help her. Now imagine walking back to your work area and continuing with your work, feeling a great sense of accomplishment that the situation was resolved without any violence.

Stage 6: Remember to pre-play your mental movie prior to situations happening. We are the only creature with this ability. Re-play positive outcomes and never re-play negative outcomes of real situations unless you change the outcome.

You can do this in ANY situation where you might feel threatened. If it happened once in your workplace, it might happen again. If someone relates a threatening situation to you, that they lived through, you can write the movie how you'd want it to come out if you were involved. Same with any threatening situation you've seen in the news. You can program yourself to automatically choose that personal safety habit, and take action that you've pre-played in your mind. Remember: when you visualize, you're training your mind and your body. Commit to it, repeat it over and over and over so it becomes automatic. Once it's a habit, it resides in the storehouse of your non-conscious mind.

The ability to pre-play situations in our mind's eye is absolutely amazing, and we also have the ability to replay. Remember that when you replay, *never* replay negative outcomes unless you change the outcome of the situation. You can replay the incident, but change the outcome to your liking.

Our ability to develop awareness starts with responsibility. You have to take responsibility for your thoughts, words, feelings, and actions, that's the beginning. Now break the word "responsible" down into two words: "response-able." Are you response able? Are you responsible in preparing yourself? Are you responsible in playing mental movies in case you might be involved in a situation?

What's the best way to sabotage your awareness? Talking on a cell phone? Looking through your bag while walking down the street? Digging in your pocket for something, not paying attention to the people around you? Any of those things will affect your awareness of your surroundings.

But the best way to sabotage your awareness—or the worst way, really—is to be intoxicated. If you are under the influence of drugs or alcohol, your conscious mind isn't functioning correctly, your non-conscious mind isn't functioning correctly, and you're disconnected from the universal mind. You cannot make good, safe decisions about your own safety if you cannot think straight. Steve is a friend of mine who spent twenty-six years as a police officer in northern California, and he has dozens of stories of people becoming victims simply because they let their awareness drop when they were drunk or high. A woman who, after a night of cocktails with friends, took a shortcut back to her car through an alley. She was abducted and assaulted for six hours. Another woman who hopped on a motorcycle outside a bar with someone she'd just met. He took her home, where she was beaten and sexually assaulted by several men—but she survived the vicious assault. A fifteen-year-old girl whom Steve repeatedly picked up in a dangerous part of town. Several times, he drove her home, to her nice, upscale neighborhood. He warned her and her grandparents about what she was doing (she had obvious puncture marks in her arm). Unfortunately, she was far more interested in getting her hands on the drugs that were available in that bad neighborhood, than staying safe. A few weeks after he first encountered her, she was found beaten to death in a parking lot.

Of course, these people were not responsible for the vicious crimes they were victims of. But had she *not* been drunk, that woman wouldn't have cut through that alley. The other woman probably wouldn't have taken off on a Harley with someone she had just met. Without her thinking muddied from drug use, that sad, tragic fifteen-year-old girl would never have been in a part of town where murder was all too commonplace.

These are extreme examples, but think of how many times you have let your awareness drop because you'd had a few? Of course, I'm not saying "never drink," but make safe choices *before* you drink. Have a plan to get home safely—whether it's from a bar, an office party, a friend's house, whatever. Take responsibility so you are able to respond when you need to.

Unfortunately, almost any workplace, any restaurant, any theater can have a threatening situation. Your responsibility for yourself and your safety might involve playing mental movies, taking certain precautions, being aware. It all starts with responsibility. Pay attention. Pay attention to what's going on inside of you and outside of you, that's part of our awareness, self-awareness, situational awareness. Begin with that, paying attention, focusing on internal and external thoughts and inputs, messages that we receive continuously. Be present. The beauty of being present is that we don't have to keep our minds constantly busy thinking about all the possible things that can go amiss—that is counter-productive, and we'll talk more about that in Chapter 2. Just be present, be in the moment.

Gavin de Becker, an internationally known celebrity protection expert, talks about being present in his newest book, *Just 2 Seconds: Using Time and Space to Defeat Assassins.* In this compendium of assassination attempts on political figures and celebrities over the last couple of hundred years, de Becker explains what "being present" really means. He breaks down the word "present" into two words, "pre" and "sent." When we are pre-sent, we are actually ahead of time, as Gavin explains. So be "pre sent" in your ability to develop your awareness, live in the moment, be in the right now. (We'll get more in-depth about this and how it relates to defending yourself, in Chapter 5.) That will keep your awareness at its utmost, at its keenest ability. Be proactive. Proactive individuals recognize the importance of responsibility and awareness. Being proactive means you don't blame, complain, shame, or justify—you take responsibility. Attitude is everything, it really is. Your success with everything you do depends on your attitude. Creating a positive attitude about life and all the events you experience will help develop and enhance your awareness.

"We can never relax our vigilance about crime, about enforcement, about prevention. There's going to be some new problem down the road."

— Janet Reno, first woman Attorney General of the United States

Chapter 2

Vigilance

The white-tailed deer of North America is a perfect example of vigilance. You usually only see them in the early morning or evening (occasionally, they come out during the day), when it's safest for them. And when they're out, it's usually because they're feeding.

If you watch one feed, you'll see the deer put its head down, take some bites of grass or leaves, then bring its head up and look around. It's probably an unconscious, habitual thing that white-tailed deer do. They'll eat, come up, and as they're chewing they're looking around, looking for danger, for threats, for things that can hurt them. They're very aware of their surroundings, they use their senses, and they have an alert system—that white tail comes up like a big flag that alerts other deer of danger or threat.

Vigilance is part of your awareness. I define it as: *the process of paying attention to your internal and external messages with regards to other people and yourself.* What takes you out of vigilance is distraction.

Vigilance, NOT Paranoia

I want to be really, really clear about something. When I talk about awareness and vigilance, I am NOT talking about hyper-vigilance. I am NOT talking about being scared, paranoid, startling easily. Hyper-vigilance is a negative condition. It's maintaining an abnormal awareness of your environmental stimuli that causes anxiety, and can lead to mental and physical exhaustion.

People often get confused here. When I say, "Be aware, be vigilant," they think that they need to scan their environment all the time, look in the bushes, look everywhere to be ready in case something does happen. That's not it at all. That takes you away from your ability to perceive dangers and threat. You're overloading your conscious mind with irrelevant details, and you may not even recognize danger signals from your nonconscious mind, or the universal mind.

Being vigilant just means that you're in the moment, you're in the now, that you allow those messages to come freely, whether they're external or internal, you're just allowing.

Hypervigilance is a negative condition which you should avoid. It's a matter of taking – taking in the information, analyzing it, and letting it go. If it's not a threat, not a danger, then let it go. Don't let that distract you. Don't let that take you out of your ability to stay in this optimum sense of awareness by being in a state of vigilance.

Think of all the war movies you've seen. There's always the one soldier who's jumping at shadows, pointing his gun every which way. He's sweating, he's breathing hard, he jumps three feet in the air if someone taps him on the shoulder. Doesn't that guy usually get killed? Or worse— he kills someone by accident. That's another extreme example, but it's a great illustration of how counter-productive and even dangerous hypervigilance can be.

If a squirrel came near a white-tailed deer, would it bolt? Probably not. But any human anywhere near it, and it will run away. Can you imagine what a hyper-vigilant deer would be like? It would always be running through the forest, startled by the wind in the trees. That's not natural, and it's not an effective way to keep itself safe.

Vigilance for you and me means taking reasonable precautions—like the woman who stopped parking near that shrub at her gym. Steve, my retired officer friend, taught a real estate agent a lesson in vigilance that he hopes she took to heart:

> I now live in a semi-rural, Western state. Things feel
> very small-town here, very friendly, very safe. One day I
> made arrangements to meet a real estate agent at a prop-

erty I wanted to view. It was on several acres, and the home was way back off the highway. Pretty secluded. I got there first, and got out of my truck and started looking around. A few minutes later, the real estate agent, a woman in her 30s, pulled up and hopped out of her car immediately. She walked right up to me and introduced herself, then led me toward the house. I said to her, "Ma'am, do you know me?" She looked confused and looked at her clipboard, and said, "Aren't you Steve?" I said, "Yeah, but how do YOU know that?" She still looked confused, so I pulled out my ID, showing that I was who I said I was, and asked her, "Does anyone from your office know you're out here?" She said, "Uh, no. I don't think so." I asked her, "Do you think that's safe? To meet someone out at a secluded property, with no one knowing where you were going, or who you were going to meet?" She looked really taken aback, and said, "Well, what should I do? I have to meet clients." So I told her, "At a minimum, make sure someone in your office knows what property you're showing, who you're meeting, and when you're meeting them. As you pull up, you should be ON your cell phone, with a co-worker, a relative, a friend, anyone. Give them the license plate of your client's vehicle before you exit your own vehicle, then stay on your phone as you get out of the car, and give them a physical description of the person or people you're meeting. ASK FOR ID. Your client should have ID, and you need to make sure you're getting the right name. If they won't show you ID, that's a red flag. Leave."

I don't know if she followed that advice or not. But now, at least she knows how to be safer in those situations.

Again, this is vigilance and awareness, not hyper-vigilance and paranoia. A woman meeting a man alone needs to put her safety ahead of worrying about making someone feel uncomfortable because you're asking for ID, or taking down their license plate number. If she *did* face a client who was offended, she could always explain that's it's standard operating procedure when meeting a new client.

Dangerous Distractions

Distractions take you away from your ability to be vigilant. Distractions can be internal and external. Internal distractions are your thoughts—thinking about something that's going to happen, thinking about something that already happened, worrying about your kids, money, your spouse, etc. External distractions are noises, the TV, radio, kids in the backseat chattering, your phone ringing, your computer beeping at you. Lights can be distractions; flashing, bright, anything that grabs your attention.

Distractions usually work on your visual sense or auditory sense, and they're everywhere. They take you away from your focus, your intention, your attention and your ability to stay aware of your environment, to live in the now, and to be in the moment. When you're distracted, your awareness or vigilance is impaired, and your guard comes down. Again, I'm not talking about having your guard up all the time, feeling scared and paranoid. But when you're distracted, just like when you're hyper-vigilant, you may miss signals from your non-conscious mind or the universal mind. Again, being vigilant means being present, being here, paying attention to external and internal distractions.

Sensing Your World

You communicate with the external world through your five senses. Your five senses also keep you safe, which you learned as a child. I know when I was a little kid, and I touched the wood stove and it was hot, it burned my fingers. That taught me that it's dangerous, and not to do that. A lot of us learned that lesson the hard way, with burnt fingers from a burner, a candle, the iron, etc.

Your sense of hearing often gives you the first alert that something's wrong—a shriek, a scream, your dog barking, a siren that's getting closer. Sometimes in the middle of the night you might hear something disturbing, that creaking sound you know is not normal, because your non-conscious mind wakes you up, that that sound is not right. So that alerts you to this potential danger and gets you ready, prepares you.

You probably don't think of your sense of taste keeping you safe, but have you ever taken a bite of something and you knew it just wasn't right? Maybe this food has something noxious or pungent about it, and the bite of food you just took told you that it wasn't right for your system? Or even spoiled? I'm not talking about that broccoli soup or the Brussels sprouts you hated as a kid, I'm talking about that real sense of something not right with this food, and it makes you want to spit it out of your mouth. In this day and age, it's probably a sense we use less, when we get all our food from a grocery store, than we did thousands of years ago, when we had to figure out what was safe to eat, but it's still a part of how we interact with and perceive the world around us.

Your sense of smell can alert you to noxious fumes, smoke, blood, things like that. It can also tell you if someone is under the influence. You can smell that on them, alerting you that there's a potential threat or danger here.

Sight is one of our most powerful senses. Sight is how you first evaluate others: their body language, their facial expressions, their eye communication, if they're posturing. It gives you immediate signals of potential danger. Law enforcement and security officers know that. The power of observation can keep you safe.

What About That *Other* Sense?

Is there a sixth sense? I'm talking about that ability that we all have to sense something that we can't see, we can't hear, we can't feel, we can't touch, something beyond your five senses. I call it intuition. There are other names for it, but we'll stick with intuition for now.

Intuition is knowing without knowing why. It's like a security system that is always on and ever vigilant, surveying not only danger but everything else as well. It communicates to you through symbols, feelings, and even your emotions. It's radar for sensing, seeing or feeling danger before it is present. Have you ever known that the teacher was going to call on you before the teacher actually did? Have you ever been thinking about a particular person, and all of a sudden, the phone rings, and it's that person? Have you ever had the phone ring, and before you picked up the receiver or glanced at caller ID, you knew exactly who it was? Here's one almost everyone can relate to: have you ever been thinking about a particular song that you hadn't heard in a long time? As it's running through your head, you get in your car, you turn your radio on and that song is playing?

Have you ever encountered a person who just didn't seem right, just gave you an uneasy feeling? You didn't know him from Adam, but something wasn't right about this person. It caused you to pause, caused you to hesitate, and reevaluate what was around you, what was going on with this particular person. I'll bet you can think of a lot of different times in your life when you were proven right: that nice, quiet co-worker who was stealing the company blind. Or that neighbor who was hitting his kids, but was always pleasant socially. We've all been there. We all understand this intuitive feeling. Some of us brush it off as "women's intuition" or "a hunch," but when we do get it and we get a strong "gut feeling," we should trust those feelings. A neighbor told me this story:

> When my son was two, my husband rented an office in a building that had several other offices. We got to know one of his "work neighbors" in the building fairly well. One day my son and I were visiting my husband at work, and, as it happened, there were several of us standing around in the foyer, just chatting. Suddenly, I realized I couldn't see my son. I had no idea where he was. I didn't panic right away, I just started looking for him and calling his name. After a minute or so, as I *was* starting to panic, that neighbor came around a corner, holding my son's hand. I went *ballistic*. I went off on that man like I have never done before, screaming at him, using foul language, that he had no right to take my child out of my sight, that it was my job to keep him safe. I got up in his face and told him if he *ever* came near my child again I would rip him apart. Now, I am 5'1", I weigh about 100 pounds, and I am a pre-school teacher. I have a VERY soft voice. I had *never* spoken to anyone like that in my life. My husband was mortified. Everyone standing around stared at me open-mouthed. The

guy just backed up with his hands up, and walked away. When I calmed down, in the car on the way home, even *I* was embarrassed, but I refused to apologize, and my husband let it drop. I didn't know why I had had such a violent reaction, but I knew I was right. Well, about ten years later, we saw in the paper that that guy had been arrested for molesting little boys.

Trust your gut feelings, trust your hunches, trust your intuition. That sixth sense will keep you and your loved ones safe.

Practice Makes Improvement

Desmond Morris, an English zoologist, wrote a book called *Body Talk: The Meaning of Human Gestures.* In his book, he lists more than fifty body signals or messages that are universal to all human beings in every culture. The majority of these messages are communicated unconsciously, so we're unaware of using them. Just as the communication of these messages is unconscious, so is your ability to read these non-verbal communication signals.

If I asked you to write out a dozen of these non-verbal messages, you might get eight, nine, ten, maybe even twelve: smile, frown, eyes wide, hands out with palms up, etc. But if you had to write out all fifty, could you? You'd probably struggle; I know I would. But all of us, regardless of our culture, respond and understand these messages intuitively. It's a safeguard. Someone holds up a hand, palm out, it means stop. Someone beckons to you, it means come. Everyone understands these, so verbal communication isn't always required.

The trick to using intuition more effectively is to bring the unconscious data that it supplies to a place where your conscious mind can interpret it, and we all have this ability. Are women better at intuition than men? Often, yes. But it's not that women are gifted with this ability more than men—they just trust it more than men do. And I think it's a maternal thing. Women have to communicate with their babies, who can't communicate with language until they're at least one to two years old. But how does a mom communicate with her newborn baby? She communicates intuitively, and the baby communicates intuitively as well. Moms, you can tell when your baby is happy, or sad, or hungry. And us dads tap into this a little bit too, but I think moms tap into it a lot more, because moms are usually the primary caregivers of our infants.

Continuous messages come to you all the time, and some of these messages are mundane messages, like "The light is green. Press the accelerator." Occasionally, they are very threatening or dangerous messages. I think it's important to understand an order or ranking of the types of messages you get to help keep you safe. I call these the messages of intuition.

I was just thinking about her...

The first message of intuition I described is that phone call. You know, you're thinking about your mom, sure enough the phone rings and it's her, or you know who's on the phone prior to picking it up. This is called *synchronicity*. That word was coined by Carl Jung, the Swiss psychologist, who defined synchronicity as the inner connectedness of all things. We've all had those moments, those incidents, those situations that were synchronistic— we just knew. That's the connectedness of you and other people or events and things.

I can't shake this feeling ...

The second messenger is *nagging feelings*. Have you ever had those nagging feelings about someone, something, a certain situation, and it caused you to reevaluate before you actually made that purchase, got in that car, or made a decision because of that nagging feeling? It's like the mother who has a nagging feeling that her teenage son's friend is bad news—no matter how polite he seems—and it turns out the kid is into drugs, or stealing, or worse.

I'll bet that guy's not telling the truth.

Hunches are the next messenger of intuition. People often get hunches about something, and then they follow it, and get what they want—or they don't follow it and wish they had. My good friend Brian is a private investigator who specializes in surveillance. Insurance companies hire him to follow people whom they suspect of worker's comp fraud; that is, someone who says she hurt her back really badly at work, but gets caught on tape moving heavy furniture, chopping wood, whatever. So Brian is the guy in that van with the dark windows, who sits in parking lots or down the street and gets video of the person who filed the claim. It's perfectly legal, and Brian is really good at catching those people who are ballroom dancing when they claim they can't walk. Brian tells me that when he trusts his hunch, he's almost always right; he thinks it's at least 95% of the time. So, when he follows the hunch, he gets a better lead, he gets a better take on the investigation. That saves him time, which saves him money.

I have another friend who has told me that every time she ignores her hunch, she regrets it. Now she always trusts her hunches, and she hardly ever gets caught in traffic, she can always find a parking space, the store always has exactly what she's looking for—and, she claims, it's usually on sale.

I don't know why, but I just feel it in my gut.

The next message of intuition is one of my favorites. It's called *the gut feeling*. Nagging feelings are things that give you time to think. Hunches are thoughts that cross your mind. But gut feelings are just that: a visceral experience, in your gut, telling you the right answer. Ever had that gut feeling, something isn't right? You know, something is going to go wrong, something about this particular person—it's that gut feeling. It's almost that it's inside of us. My gut is just telling me that it just isn't right. Police talk about gut feelings all the time—maybe a suspect who has an alibi that checks out *at first*, but the officer knows something is off, and finds out the alibi is a lie.

Gut feelings are called that for a reason: it often feels like a rock in your gut, sometimes even like a blow to your gut. But you feel it right there in the center of your body, where you can't—or at least, you shouldn't—ignore it.

He *sounds* sincere, but I just don't know.

The next messages of intuition are *hesitation and doubt*. I'm not talking about second-guessing yourself constantly. There's a difference between lacking confidence in your decisions, or lacking confidence in a person, and truly feeling hesitation or doubt. Have you ever had someone tell you a story, and your first thought is, "No way that's true," when there really isn't any evidence it's a lie? Or you *almost* buy that used car on the spot, because it's exactly what you're looking for—but something holds you back. So you go home and check the VIN, and you find out that it was in a bad accident. Those are the times these messengers of intuition are at work.

I don't trust her. I just don't.

Another message of intuition is *suspicion*. A lot of police officers that I know use this message of intuition as their guide in investigations, solving crimes, and preventing crimes. They just have a suspicious nature about them anyway when it comes to protecting you and protecting society. When it's hot out, a guy in a heavy overcoat is always suspicious. But if other indicators tell you he's homeless, and non-threatening, you let it go. If that same guy is sweating and looking around nervously, he may be hiding something dangerous under that coat. Peace officers are trained to be suspicious about things, and occasionally that message of suspicion is overwhelming and they take action on it, and prevent a dangerous situation.

Why is the hair on the back of my neck standing up?

The next message of intuition is *physical changes*. I mean physical changes in you. This is when something just isn't right and you know it. You might not know it on a conscious level, but your non-conscious mind knows it, so it starts to prepare the body, getting ready to either fight, or take flight. You get goose bumps, the hair on the back of your neck stands up, you tense up, your heart rate increases, so does your blood pressure, your respiration changes. These are all physical changes the body goes through as it prepares to protect itself. And it's all done on a non-conscious level. Pretty amazing.

WATCH OUT!

The most urgent message of intuition is that knowingness that there is clear danger. A situation, an event, a person is dangerous, and you know it, you know it with all of your being. And when that happens, most of us take immediate action and we do something.

Through these different messages, your intuition is always communicating to you. Sometimes your primal instinct overreacts and sends unnecessary danger signals. People suffering from PTSD will often get a much stronger danger sense than is warranted in a situation. But everything your intuition communicates to you is meaningful in some way, form, or fashion.

I don't trust that guy, but I don't want to hurt his feelings.

The enemy of intuition, which bogs you down, is worry. When we start to worry, it means we're thinking about the past or the future, which takes you away from being in the present moment where intuition communicates to you most effectively. Remember my neighbor who unwittingly protected her son from a child molester? I asked her if she was worried about his reaction to her tirade:

> No. Which I remember I thought was strange, at the time. While I was getting in his face, I did not worry for one second "how it looked" or if I was embarrassing him or myself. All I knew was I needed to be absolutely sure he never came near my son again.

Intuition might send any of several messages to get your attention, and because they differ in accordance to urgency, it's good to understand this particular hierarchy. If you bypass nagging feelings, hunches, hesitation, doubt or a gut feeling and go right to physical changes, you need to acknowledge it. Not try to step back and rationalize it. If my neighbor had tried to rationalize her verbal attack on that pedophile, she might not have been as forceful to scare him away from her son.

Hone Your Skills

There's a way to get better at recognizing when your intuition is at work, and to practice using your intuition, honing it to improve your ability to stay safe.

Intuition is the original communication system used by humans long before we had spoken language. It's your ability to read a person's attitudes and thoughts by their behaviors. Have you ever been driving along on the freeway, and you don't even know why, but you turn your head, and you look at the car next to you? And what are they doing? Sure enough, they're looking at you, aren't they? It happens all the time. Most of the time we're just not aware of it, or we don't pay attention. This is what I call the inner connectedness, this conduit that connects all human beings. This knowledge of this sixth sense, that somebody is looking at you, your ability to pay attention to that, helps you stay safe.

Often when a person looks at another person, it's unconscious. Probably like the white-tailed deer, just looking around, checking things out. But sometimes, there is some intention behind it, and we can read that intention from people. If a person is looking at you and they've got bad intentions, you can perceive that. You can be aware of it, and make a decision to get away from them, to do something about it.

We all have this intuitive capability to know when another person is looking at us. Like all intuitive messages, it's just a matter of paying attention, recognizing it, and when it happens, make a conscious statement to yourself, "My intuitive ability is getting better all the time." And as it gets better all the time, then change that statement to, "My intuition is excellent. I'm an intuitive person." By claiming this, making a declaration that you are intuitive, it makes your intuitive ability even stronger so that if potentially dangerous things happen, or synchronistic situations come up, you track on that, you'll get better and better at your ability to recognize, trust and use your intuition to stay safe.

Can you remember a time when you had an intuitive feeling about something that you disregarded? Maybe you just ignored it, or you went along with someone else's feelings or their opinion. How did that work for you? How did you feel afterwards? How did things work out?

When you listen to, trust, and act on your intuitive and inner guidance, it becomes an art. Like any art or discipline, it requires a commitment. It's an ongoing awareness which challenges you to develop a deeper understanding of your own personal self-awareness. Using your intuition means that you learn to read other people's body language. When you do that, it teaches you to be aware of their behaviors, their intentions, and ultimately their motives. I'll use the saying "stop, look and listen" to help you develop your ability to be intuitive. Developing and using your vigilance means that you need to stop, look and listen occasionally to what your feelings are telling you, what your senses are telling you, your perceptions and the context of particular situations that are going on are telling you at that present moment. If it doesn't feel right, it probably isn't.

My two daughters are almost grown now, but I taught them a long time ago to trust their perception of what's happening, to trust their intuition. Several years ago, I'd just gotten back from a work trip. My daughters were young at the time, probably eight and twelve, and they were outside playing. My younger daughter was kicking a soccer ball around outside, and her sister was practicing some cheerleading moves. As I walked past them, they gave me hugs, and I walked inside and set my luggage down inside the door. A moment later, my older daughter ran in. I thought it was strange, and she had a look on her face that just wasn't right. I just looked at her for a second, trying to read her expression. Something told me to walk outside, so I did.

Out in front of my house, a middle-aged guy had pulled up in an older car. I didn't recognize him or his car. He had gotten out of his car, and walked up to my younger daughter, and she didn't really know what to do. She was just kind of walking towards the neighbor's house. This had all transpired in just thirty seconds, maybe a minute or so. But this guy had pulled up and was asking my two daughters if they had seen his lost puppy. I immediately confronted this guy and said, no, we hadn't seen any lost puppies. I also told him I didn't think it was smart of him to approach my young daughters like that. That's one of the tell-tale signs of sexual predators, to approach kids and ask for the lost puppy or the lost cat. And, in my opinion, he was being rude, and shouldn't have approached my kids.

I can't be sure what his intentions were, whether they were malicious or not. (But you'd think any adult male in this day and age would know that was inappropriate behavior.) He knew from my body language and tone to leave immediately. We took his license plate down and reported it to the sheriff's department.

I got my daughters inside and we sat down and talked about what had just happened. They both knew that it just didn't feel right, and that's why my older daughter had come inside with that strange look on her face and why my younger daughter had started to walk towards the neighbor's house. So my guidance to them was, first of all, trust your intuition. Second, I explained that a better choice would have been that they both came inside our house immediately, and told me exactly what was going on. As for me, if I'd stopped my daughter, and asked for an explanation why she came inside, it would have left enough time for that guy to grab my other daughter, if that *had* been his intention. So I trusted my intuition, and I went outside immediately. I reminded them that they were both right to trust their intuition that if it doesn't feel right, it isn't right, so trust that! Trust that ability that we all have. Listen to that inner guidance. That's what intuition, that's what vigilance, does for us.

When you worry, when you're thinking about the future or thinking about the past, it takes you away from that ability to be the safe, and that is your intuitive guidance system. Be *aware* of what is going on around you and inside of you. Be *vigilant* in recognizing your intuition, and you will be safe.

"The best self-defense is to not be there when the attack takes place."
— David Fowler

Chapter 3

Avoidance

What is the best self-defense? Is it Karate, Kung fu? What about Taekwondo, mixed martial arts, ultimate fighting? Is it weapons— mace, pepper spray, guns, knives? I've asked thousands of people that very question, and the answer might surprise you, because it's not rocket science. The best self-defense is simply *not to be there* when the attack takes place. Pretty simple, pretty straightforward. It doesn't matter how many blocks, kicks, strikes, or take-downs the other guy knows. If you avoid a dangerous situation altogether, you'll never risk being assaulted or robbed—or worse.

So what does that mean in real-world circumstances? It means you use your *awareness* to know what's going on around you, to be *vigilant* about keeping yourself safe, so you *avoid* dangerous situations. Consider these five scenarios, and think about how you could use *avoidance* to keep yourself safe:

1. You're in line for a movie, outside the building. Some older teenagers, around 18 or 19, are right behind you in line, and are getting physically aggressive toward each other. One of them accidentally shoves you, but becomes belligerent as soon as you turn around. What do you do?

2. You pull into a gas station/convenience store in the middle of the day. You're talking on your cell phone, but you notice something

odd. It takes you a few seconds to put your finger on "what's wrong with this picture," but you realize there are several cars parked by the pumps, but no people around. You can't see anyone inside the store, which is all glass in the front. What do you do?

3. You're sound asleep upstairs in your home. You are woken up by a loud crash downstairs. You freeze for a moment, then you're almost certain you hear low voices and footsteps. Your spouse hears them, too. Your children are asleep in the other rooms upstairs. What do you do?

4. You're walking down a street. A guy runs past you, and grabs your briefcase/ purse/bag as he runs past. What do you do?

5. You're on the freeway, and an aggressive driver is tailing you, speeding up on you, then braking. You've seen this driver cutting in and out of traffic behind you, and he cut someone off and almost caused an accident. You can't safely slow down to let him pass in the traffic circumstances, and you're so annoyed, you want to speed up and tap your brakes to tell him to back off. What do you do?

Anyone could be in any of those situations. Think about these scenarios. Consider what you would do in each situation. We'll come back to these examples later in this chapter.

The best defenses against crime and violence are pro-active prevention, and defensive intervention, in that order. We'll talk about defensive intervention in Chapter 5, but my goal is for you never to get to that point, for you never to find yourself having to physically defend yourself or your loved ones. It's the decisions that you make, and the actions that you take—with the proper knowledge and wisdom of what to do in a threatening situation—that will be your best self-defense.

Criminal Predators

When I was a kid, every Sunday evening I would go to my grandparents' house and watch a television show with them called "Mutual of Omaha's Wild Kingdom." Remember that show? The scenes I remember most vividly are the predators stalking their prey, especially the lions and the cheetahs. They would camouflage themselves in the grass, and they would quietly sneak up on their prey (impala, wildebeest, whatever was available). But they would sneak very calmly, very quietly, using all their senses, watching, smelling, listening. Once they got close enough, they'd wait for the right moment, then they would attack. Often, they would corral the herd, then split the herd to separate the weak, the old, and the young. Predators always go for the easiest kill.

Human predators have one thing in common with animal predators: they will go for the easiest target. Human predators will use any environment, any camouflage, any tools at their disposal. In the animal kingdom, the predator usually has to be stronger or faster than its prey. Unfortunately, human predators have ways to equal the playing field, things animals don't have: weapons, fear, intimidation, etc. Most crime and violence occur during evening and nighttime hours, but some predators choose daytime simply because people are more likely to let their guard down.

Who commits crime and violence? People do. People from all walks, genders, races, ethnicities and social positions. The only things that separate one person from another are their choices and values. Some people choose to make choices that hurt other people. To be safe, you need to choose to be aware and be vigilant.

Don't Be Preyed Upon

After studying human predators, I've learned there's a strong correlation between predators in the animal world and human predators in our society. Do predators look for certain characteristics that prey display? They certainly do. The predator doesn't want someone who's going to resist, so they select prey that is old, weak, young and even distracted.

Let's look at the characteristics of people as potential prey, what they show, and how they act. There are five different types of human prey:

Unconsciously Un-Aware: Someone who is "clueless". With women, I see this a lot when they are unaware a man is watching them, even if it's some place seemingly harmless, like in a restaurant.

Un-Prepared: A higher state of conscious awareness than unconsciously un-aware, but lacking in preparedness of potential situations. For instance, walking up to your front door, and *then* trying to dig out your house key. Why not sit in your well-lit car a moment longer, and get your house key out and ready? You don't have those mental plans for potential situations that you may encounter.

Un-Secured: Not using the precautionary security tools and equipment in your different environments. Some people who live in apartment buildings like to prop open the security door because it might be a pain to buzz people in, or walk down and let them in. Does that sound smart?

Consciously Un-Aware: A dangerous state of denial; the "nothing can happen to me" mentality. "I don't need to lock my car/my house." "I know that ATM is poorly lit, but I'll be fine."

Un-Fortunate: Being in the wrong place at the wrong time. But this is usually the least likely event to happen. Most often prey are unaware, un-prepared, and un-secured.

Predators learn how to adapt so that they can get their prey. They learn how to be faster and use their senses to look for opportune times. They learn to adapt as a survival mechanism. Prey also learn how to adapt as a survival mechanism, so that they could evolve and live. But just because you're not a predator does *not* automatically make you prey. *Don't be prey.* Adapt, and learn to identify predators and learn to *avoid* them.

Don't Be an Easy Target

Adaptive traits that you can use to avoid and survive predators can be structural, behavioral, psychological and even physiological.

Structural Adaptations: Lock Your Doors! Structural adaptations are things like locking your doors, your windows, your car. At work, you might need to key in or scan a card to get in. Security alarms, CCTV, motion sensors, these are all things that keep you safe and are structurally adaptive devices in our lives. I'm not saying you need to run out and buy an expensive burglar alarm, but lock your doors. Even when you're home. Unfortunately, attackers are getting more and more brazen, and daytime crime is getting more common.

Behavioral Adaptations. In this book, you will learn to recognize threatening behaviors in others[4]. But more importantly, you need to adapt your behavior to be less of an attractive target. Be a hard target.

Don't stand out. Behave in ways that do not cause unwanted attention. Do you stand out or call unwanted attention to yourself? When traveling overseas, for example, you want to blend in with your environment. Wearing flashy jewelry or flashing wads of cash around calls a lot of attention. That stands out. That will call attention to you and put you at bigger risk of being a victim.

Walk strong. Presence can be a big deterrent. We'll cover the importance of presence more in-depth later in this chapter, but a predator is looking for the weak, the timid, the shy, the distracted. If you're posture is erect, you're confident. You just can't help but feel more confident when you get your shoulders back. That's why your parents said, "Stop slumping! Stand up straight." A slumped posture shows that you are unaware, that you're an easy target. Have a confident stride, arms swaying back and forth, head up, eyes up, looking around you. You've seen the opposite of that, right? The unconfident, easy-target stride is somewhat lackadaisical, kind of dragging their feet. They look like they won't put up a fight.

A meek presence is just the opposite of an assertive presence. It says, "I'm submissive, I'm weak, I'm an easy target."

Be aware. Be aware of your surroundings. If a predator sees that you're aware, he will be less likely to choose you as his prey. But if you're busy on your phone, listening to music, you've got your iPod on, are you aware of your surroundings? Are you living in the moment? Be present. Be aware.

Are your actions purposeful? Are they specific? If you stride up to the ATM confidently, card in hand, looking around you, you look prepared and aware. That sends a message of confidence. When your actions are non-specific it sends the opposite message, that you're an easy target. Walking up to the ATM, still on the phone, digging in your wallet or bag for your ATM card.

Stay out of dangerous places and dangerous situations! When you're leaving work, walk out to the parking lot or parking structure with a buddy. Always carry a cell phone. Tell friends, family or co-workers

---

[4] You'll learn more about that in Chapter 4.

where you are going, and when you expect to be back. If you work late, don't walk out to your car alone. Men, even you can be attacked and robbed, and your car stolen. If you're getting gas in an area you're not familiar with, make sure it's a well-lit parking lot. *Be aware.* Don't blindly wander into dangerous situations.

Sometimes going to a bar, club or party sounds like a great idea. Then you get there, and realize it's just not safe. Leave. Immediately. You can have fun somewhere that doesn't feel unsafe.

A predator is an opportunist. If they get their prey alone, that's an opportunity for them. Any predator wants to isolate their prey from others. Isolation gives the predator advantage and keeps him/her away from unwanted attention.

Never allow yourself to be isolated, confined or trapped, never allow that. Don't get in a car with someone you don't know. If you are forced into a car, you've got some choices: you can resist, or submit. Studies have shown that whether people resist or submit, the injury rate is almost identical. I know for me personally that if I end up in a situation where I am isolated, confined or trapped, my choice based on preparing myself and my awareness and playing that mental movie is that I'm not going—I'm personally not going to submit, I'm going to resist. But it's a personal choice and one that should be evaluated. And I can't give you any absolute answers for that— should you submit or should you resist, it just all depends on your self-awareness and personal readiness.

Alcohol and drugs will impair your awareness, making you vulnerable. If you're in a situation where a lot of people are drinking, you have to be careful. People often get more violent when they're intoxicated; conversely, being drunk makes you an easy target[5]. If you know you're impaired from drinking, have a friend help you get home. If that drunk guy at the party is scaring you or making you uncomfortable, *leave.* No matter how big and strong you are, once you're intoxicated, you just became easy prey. Stay aware, so you stay safe.

---

[5] According to the University of Illinois at Urbana-Champaign, Women's Programs, "Research indicates that as many as half of all rapes are committed by males who have been drinking. Similarly, about half of the women who are raped have also been drinking." http://www.odos.uiuc.edu/women/support/sexualAssault/alcohol.asp

Psychological Adaptation: Change Your Mindset. All those behavioral adaptations we just talked about start right here, with your psychological adaptations. To *avoid* predators, you have to be *aware* and *vigilant*. Trust those internal and external messages to help keep you safe. By being aware and being vigilant, you'll avoid a lot of danger.

Physiological Adaptation: Be Able to Protect Yourself. Physiological adaptation is your self-awareness of your physical ability and your ability to defend yourself or take action. If you have the ability to run, and you're aware of it, you know that you can get away, it helps give you the confidence to overcome an attacker. For me, the ability to defend myself with martial arts or defensive intervention techniques is my physiological ability to adapt and to overcome.

You can learn all these adaptations to make yourself safe. It doesn't mean you have to install an expensive burglar alarm in your house, or become a black belt in Karate. But think through all those adaptations listed—are you doing everything you can, with what you have now, to be as safe as possible?

If not, how can you improve? And remember—the MOST important thing in staying safe is your mindset.

The Reverse Line-Up

A typical police line-up is done with suspects being lined up and the victim determining if any of the suspects in the line-up are the perpetrator of the crime. The reverse line-up is just the opposite; the line-up is everyday people in everyday life, and the predator determines the prey he/she will select from that line-up. So what if, in a reverse line up, the predators are evaluating and selecting their prey, which is US?

Are there messages that we send unconsciously or even consciously that a predator might pick up out of a line-up (society) that shows we may be easy prey? Do you send unconscious messages that you are afraid and weak? And the biggest question is, can you change those unconscious messages? The answer is YES, you can—through your awareness, vigilance and avoidance.

The Power of Intention

A person's intentions are a reflection of their thoughts coming from their face, body posture, the position of their hands and from the way they wear their clothes, their dress. Intentions can also show an individual's level of confidence, their emotional state and their motives and attitudes. Understanding the characteristics of predators coupled with your awareness and vigilance will alert you to a person's intentions. Remember, if it doesn't feel right, it probably isn't.

I believe that we all have the ability to sense another's intentions. It's even more than what you can observe about them; it's where that sixth sense comes into play. A smile can be inviting—or terrifying. Somehow, you *know* the difference; you just have to trust yourself.

Can you recall a time when you are aware of a person's intentions or motives? What was it that they did or they said or that you saw in them that told you what their intentions were? Were their intentions good? Were they bad? What was that feeling that you had about this person's intentions? Could you see it or could you just feel it?

When I was a full-contact fighter, my coach, Marc Costello, would tell me, "Dave, when you get into the ring, you better have the intention of winning, of doing what you need to do to your opponent." In the full-contact Karate arena, the intentions that I needed were to dominate, to win, to overcome my opponent. I always set those intentions, for each fight, and I almost always won.

What are your intentions? What messages are you sending right now? Do you send confidence? Or are you sending a message that you're weak, that you're easy, that you're prey? Are you sending those intentions with your face, your body, your façade, your posture, the position of your hands and your dress, the way you wear your clothes? What about your awareness? Are your intentions being sent correctly, to show that you're aware? Are your intentions positive or are they negative?

You have the ability to change your intentions and it all starts with our thoughts. Right now, make a conscious choice to change your intentions, to change your thoughts. Choose to be aware, be vigilant, and avoid danger.

AVOIDANCE

Presence Is Everything

Police and security all understand that they have to have a confident presence or they will not be taken seriously, they will not be able to do their job effectively. For us civilians, there are three different levels of safety presence: confident presence, assertive presence, and defensive presence.

A confident presence, again, means that you're aware. You're aware of your environment. It's not that you're hyper-vigilant, you're not paranoid or scared, you're just aware. That sends a message to people around you that you're confident. What you do with your eyes, how you look at people is a message of a confident presence.

Assertive presence is part of your interaction with other people. There are times when you have to be assertive. It means that you're standing behind your belief systems, and your belief systems are based on your upbringing, your moral and ethical understanding of life, and there are times when you have to say no to people. There are times when you have to stand up for your rights, and that is being assertive.

When you're assertive, your posture automatically gets more erect. You look people directly in the eye. You might put your hand out, with your palm facing out towards them, which is the universal sign for stop. You might put one hand up, you might put both hands up. It sends the message, "Don't get near me. Don't even think about it."

I teach nurses to send an assertive message to aggressive patients, to set limits, to enforce those limits to set the boundaries. I teach them to establish rules with their palms facing downwards. I encourage them to move their hands up and down, palms facing down, to emphasize their point; it's how you can tell someone to calm down without saying, "Calm down."

The defensive presence is for situations when you're involved with an aggressive individual, somebody who is being obnoxious and aggressive, and you have to defend yourself. So you already know that the best defense is to not be there, but should you be in a situation where you can't immediately get away, you might have to assume a defensive presence.

Now, the caution to this is you don't want to assume that defensive presence unless it's absolutely needed, *because it could escalate a situation if you become defensive.* I'll say that again: if you become defensive when it's not warranted, you could escalate a situation, and push the other person into *more* aggressive behavior. This is a tough call for women, especially. Ladies, you are biologically programmed to want to calm down heated situations, so women are often reluctant to do anything that might "make matters worse." Trust yourself. Read the other person, and *trust your instincts.* If that voice in your head is saying, "DANGER!" listen to it!

Defensive presence means that you angle your body slightly away from the other person, so instead of facing them head-on, you're at a 45-degree angle to them. Why do you do that? Because it protects your vulnerable line, which runs from your nose to your groin, and you want to protect that area. Should it be struck, you want to "blade" your body. Your feet are shoulder width apart and slightly staggered, you can move, you can block, you can defend, you can run away from this position.

When animals fight, they face head on, face-to-face. You want to avoid that. You want to blade your body, again, to protect yourself and to show that you are defensive. Your hands are going to come up in a bladed position. You've probably seen Karate people do this. I'm not advocating trying a Karate move; this position is just to send a message that you're not going to be a victim, that you are defensive in nature.

Then, obviously, the sooner that you can get away from a situation like this, the better. Remember, AVADE® is Awareness, Vigilance, avoidance, Defense, ESCAPE! Escape, escape, escape. As I hope I made very clear, the best escape, the best self-defense is not to be there. But you can't control every situation. We'll cover Defense more in Chapters 5 and 7.

So you always, always, always have a confident presence—always. Always. Did you get that? No matter what you're doing, have that awareness to be confident in all of your actions. The assertive presence is for situations where you need to set limits or boundaries, you need to say no, or you need to stand up for your belief system. The defensive presence is ONLY used in defensive situations, when a person is aggressive, when somebody is in your face and when you can't avoid them, you become defensive. Only then. Using defensive presence before you absolutely need to, can escalate a situation.

Cause and effect is a funny thing. Are you smiling because you're happy, or are you happy because you're smiling? It doesn't really matter.

It still has an effect on your mood. So even if you don't feel confident, bring your shoulders back, raise your head, and keep your eyes up and scan the area. Fake it 'til you make it! It doesn't matter where your confidence begins—if it begins on the outside because you're training yourself to have better posture, or if it begins on the inside, because you're changing the way you feel. Either way, walking with confidence will project confidence, and lower your chances of being a victim.

If you feel confident, more than likely you'll have your head up, your eyes up, your shoulders back and you'll walk with confidence. It's the same thing with being assertive. If you feel assertive, your body language will emanate that, will show through your body language that you're assertive. Defensiveness is the same way. Again, even if you don't feel like it, use your body language and it'll change the way you feel on the inside.

The law of cause and effect is a universal law, and just knowing that should empower you to use body language in a purposeful way to show your confidence, your assertiveness when needed, and of course your defensiveness when needed for situations that involve using defensive intervention.

Develop Your Avoidance Techniques

There are six areas that you can use to develop your avoidance ability.

Structural avoidance involves the use of any barrier, shield, device or protective layer around you. Most commonly, these are your homes, your vehicles and your workplaces, and the security that they afford you.

Behavioral avoidance involves your ability to recognize behaviors through reading body language. Trust your ability to read others, and remember that you, too, are sending a continuous message. That message can be confident, assertive, or defensive—or a message that you're weak, timid, and scared.

Psychological avoidance is your mental awareness, your ability to recognize dangers and make decisions, choices, and responses around those dangers, to keep yourself safe.

Physiological avoidance is having the ability to physically and defensively intervene in a situation. Now you know that your presence is also a physiological deterrent, sending a message that you're not going to be a victim.

Environmental avoidance is using your safety awareness for the many different types of environments that you are in. Similar to structural avoidance but more broad in scope as your environments are broad—home, work, school, in your vehicles, in public places, etc.

Intuitive avoidance is your vigilance, which teaches you that when you are focused to receive, you will get messages internally and externally. Trusting and acting on those messages will keep you safe.

Remember those five scenarios from the beginning of the chapter? Now that you know how to avoid dangerous situations, let's look at them again.

1. You're in line for a movie, outside the building. Some older teenagers, around 18 or 19, are right behind you in line, and are getting physically aggressive toward each other. One of them accidentally shoves you, but becomes belligerent as soon as you turn around. What do you do?

Ideally, you and the rest of your party would just walk away, backing away with your palms up shows you have no intention to fight. The belligerent teen may even take it as submission, but who cares? You have nothing to prove, right? I would also report it to a manager, or even the police. If he physically shoves you intentionally, get into a bladed position, and back away as quickly as possible. Just avoid the conflict.

2. You pull into a gas station/convenience store in the middle of the day. You're talking on your cell phone, but you notice something odd. It takes you a few seconds to put your finger on "what's wrong with this picture," but you realize there are several cars parked by the pumps, but no people around. You can't see anyone inside the store, which is all glass in the front. What do you do?

Immediately—immediately—start your car and drive away. This is a perfect example of intuitive avoidance. Before you could even put your finger on it, you knew something was wrong. In that situation, definitely call the police.

3. You're sound asleep upstairs in your home. You are woken up by a loud crash downstairs. You freeze for a moment, then you're almost cer-

tain you hear low voices and footsteps. Your spouse hears them, too. Your children are asleep in the other two rooms upstairs. What do you do?

Your family has an escape plan in case of fire or intruders, right? No? We'll cover that more in Chapter 8, but what you do NOT do, is go downstairs, or call downstairs. You and your spouse each take a room with children, and get them safely out their windows. Meet back in your meeting place. If you don't have a cell phone with you, walk a few doors down, so the intruders will not hear you pounding on the next-door neighbor's front door, and call the police. Avoiding a confrontation will keep you and your family safe.

4. You're walking down a street. A guy runs past you, and grabs your briefcase/purse/bag as he runs past. What do you do?

Let go of the bag. Do not fight, do not yank on it. As one police officer told me, "I've seen more women get beaten up because whatever was in that purse was too valuable to let go of." It's not worth it. Avoid the confrontation.

5. You're on the freeway, and an aggressive driver is tailing you, speeding up on you, then braking. You've seen this driver cutting in and out of traffic behind you, and he cut someone off and almost caused an accident. You're so annoyed, you want to speed up and tap your brakes to tell him to back off. What do you do?

If at all possible, slow way down and get over so he can pass you. If you can, get his license plate and call the police. If he slows down, too, and continues to harass you, call the police immediately. Getting a ticket for being on the phone is a small price to pay. Your safety is your first priority. Get off the freeway as soon as possible, and drive to the closest police station. If you don't know where that is, ask the dispatcher on the phone—because OF COURSE, you have your cell phone in the car, and it's easy to reach, right? When you got in your car, you locked the doors, buckled your seat belt, and put your phone within easy reach in case of emergency, because you are now aware and vigilant. And, you know enough to know that avoiding possibly dangerous situations is the best thing you can do.

Avoidance is not being weak. It is not giving in. It is prioritizing your safety, and your loved ones' safety.

Whether it's your structures, your behaviors, using your mind, your psyche, your body, your physiological avoidance, the aspect of your environment or your intuitive guidance, these abilities to avoid danger, to avoid crime and violence will ultimately keep you safe. Develop your avoidance skills to keep yourself safe from predators.

"The meeting of two personalities is like the contact of two chemical substances: if there is any reaction, both are transformed."

—Carl Jung, Swiss Psychologist, 1875-1961

Chapter 4

Interpersonal Communications

Everywhere you go, you interact with people: at work, in your home, with your family members, with people out in public. In every interaction, you use your interpersonal communication skills, which you learned through your parents, at school, growing up, through all the social conditioning that you've been exposed to. Interpersonal communication is a complex and dynamic process where individuals interact with one another, usually face-to-face. Sometimes it's via electronic communication, but usually it's face-to-face. It's the way people share their ideas, their feelings, and their perceptions by simultaneously sending and receiving messages.

Messages can be exchanged verbally and non-verbally, and they may be sent intentionally or unintentionally. A situation can escalate due to poor skills—by the way someone comes across, by the way they communicate to others, through their body language. And they may be completely unconscious of it. But you have the ability to de-escalate situations based on your communication skills, too. How do you rate your ability to communicate with others on a scale of 1 to 10? Are you good? Could you be better?

In this chapter, you're going to learn to recognize when a person is escalating, when they are stressed, when they're angry, if they're intoxicated, or if they're going to be combative.

You will also learn how to de-escalate. You'll learn non-violent intervention skills, not only for recognizing, but for de-escalating those behaviors, and keeping out of the assault cycle.

Interpersonal communication skills involve listening, asserting, influencing, persuading, empathizing, sensitivity and diplomacy. Your ability to communicate with others, and effectively use these seven skills, can significantly reduce the potential for conflicts.

Active listening is a structured way of listening and responding to others. It focuses the attention on the other person. Sadly, most of us had never been through any type of education, training or seminar on listening. We're just expected to be a good listener, and retain and understand everything our spouse, boss, co-workers, kids, parents, etc., tell us. As a kindergartener you're brought into the classroom, and the teacher says sit down, be quiet and listen. But beyond that, most of us get no further training whatsoever—or, if you do, it's later on in life, in college, in the military, or workforce training. But by that point in life, you've already established some habitual responses, habitual ways of listening—and you may have bad habits. A very common bad habit is only thinking about how you're going to respond to something the person has said, rather than continuing to listen as they speak. When you're not focused on what the person is telling you, you may miss important clues or information.

Asserting is stating or expressing your positive rights, beliefs or positions. There are times in your communication process when you have to be assertive, you have to stand up for what you believe, what your position is, where you stand on a certain issue, or what your rights are. So the ability to be assertive is a major part of your interpersonal communication skills, especially when dealing with threatening or emergent situations where you have to take action immediately.

Influencing is your power to affect people, actions and events. Your ability to influence others can affect how they make decisions, if they calm down, or help you get control of the situation. It's powerful.

Persuasion, like influence, is to succeed in causing a person to do or consent to do something. So as you influence another, you persuade them to take the appropriate steps, to follow the right actions and behaviors.

Empathizing is sensing and understanding someone else's feelings as if they were your own. You've heard the old saying "put yourself in another person's shoes." Empathy is to seek first to understand, then to be understood. That is the fifth habit of *The 7 Habits of Highly Effective People*, by Stephen Covey, by the way. Your ability to empathize with another is a major asset in your communication process.

Sometimes, people get confused about the difference between sympathy and empathy. Sympathy is feeling sorry for another person, which doesn't really help a situation, because it's usually a negative feeling. But empathy means that you understand. It doesn't necessarily mean you agree, but you understand another person. If you can express that understanding to others, you can reduce the potential for escalation or conflict.

Diana Concannon, a clinical psychologist in Los Angeles, gave me a great example of sympathy versus empathy: You're walking down the street. In the street is this big hole. You fall in this hole and you can't get out. You're trapped. Somebody comes along, they look down and they see that you're trapped in this hole in the road. They jump in with you—that's sympathy.

Again, you're walking down the street. You're walking alone. There's a big hole in the street. You fall in the hole. You can't get out. You're trapped. Somebody comes along and they see that you're trapped in this hole in the street, and they throw you a rope—that's empathy. That's understanding empathy.

Sensitivity is being cognizant of, and careful about, the emotions and feelings of yourself and others. Empathy means you understand where people are coming from, what they are feeling, but sensitivity means that you are aware of another person's feelings, and you're being careful not to upset them further.

Diplomacy is having tact and skill in dealing with people. The best negotiators and salesmen are very diplomatic in their ability to close deals and to get cooperation from others. Having that tact and skill is essential in today's world, especially in dealing with situations that are potentially emergent or threatening, or dealing with people who have the potential for conflict.

What Are You REALLY Saying?

The three processes of communicating with people face-to-face are:

Nonverbal communication, such as body language, gestures, postures; *vocal communication*, which is tone and inflection; and *verbal communication*, meaning the actual words that are spoken.

Albert Mehrabian, pioneer of body language research, found that in face-to-face interaction, over half of the communication process comes through your face. In his book, *Silent Messages*, Mehrabian explains that your facial expression alone—aside from all of your other non-verbal communication— does about 55% of your communication. Your tone and inflection accounts for 38% of the communication process, and the smallest part of the communication process is in the actual words that you speak; your words only account for 7% of what you're actually saying.

Your attitudes and your emotions are continually revealed on your face, and most of us are completely unaware of it. Did you know that most people are going to form 60% to 80% of their initial opinion about a new person in just a few minutes? And where do you look at another person? You don't look at their shoes; you look at their face. That's where you start to form your initial opinion about a person. Interestingly, when I teach this to women, their almost-universal response is, "No, Dave. You're wrong. It doesn't take a few minutes to form an initial opinion of someone. It takes seconds for me to form an opinion about another person."

Think about that as you relate to others. Even though it's unconscious to you, most of your communication process is coming from your face. Are you frowning? Are you smiling? What are your eyes doing? What are your lips doing? Are they crunched up? Are they tense? Is your whole face tense? Are you looking the person in the eye? Now you have an awareness of how you're communicating. Make it a conscious awareness, and use your facial expression in an appropriate way depending on the situation.

There's no question your vocal tone matters. I know people have said things to me that just ticked me off. The words themselves weren't that bad, but the way they said it just ticked me off. It's not the words you say, it's *how* you say your words. The words themselves are important, but they're the smallest part of the equation.

You have the power to influence through your face. Smiling and laughing are universally considered to be signals that a person is happy. Smiling tells another person that you are non-threatening, and it asks them to accept you on a personal level. I've been playing with this for quite some time. I never was much of a smiler, but now when I go into the grocery store, or go into a business, I will intentionally smile at other individuals. What do most people do? They smile back at me.

The Eyes Have It

Eye communication is also important in your communication skills. I refer to the three "I's" of eye communication as: intimate, intimidating and interested. Intimate eye contact is easy to understand; remember when you fell in love, you gazed into your significant other's eyes and he or she gazed back? Or a mother stares into her baby's eyes? That's intimate eye contact. Now picture two boxers in the center of the ring for the pre-fight instruction. They're staring back at one another trying to intimidate with that long, penetrating eye contact—intimidating eye contact.

Interested eye contact is the kind that makes others feel comfortable. To build good rapport with people, maintain eye contact about two-thirds of the time. When talking, maintain eye contact approximately 40 to 60% of the time. But when you are not talking, and are actively listening to the other person, keep eye contact an average of 80% of the time. (The exception to this is in Japanese and some Asian and South American cultures where extended eye contact can be seen as aggressive or disrespectful.)

Communicate a Non-Threatening Message

What you're thinking is reflected in your body language, but your body language can also work through the law of cause and effect. Remember, when you consciously use positive body language, your attitude will change; you can't help but feel better when you smile, right? If you feel like a situation is escalating, like an anxious person is getting angry, smile. It can defuse a situation.

When listening to another person, if you lean in slightly, it shows your empathy, it shows that you're listening and you're sensitive to another person, even being diplomatic with them. When you speak, use an appropriate posture, stand straight up.

The head nod is almost universally used to indicate "yes" or agreement with another person. Using a triple head nod can be a persuasion tool to get a person to agree with you. Research shows that people will talk three to four times more than usual when the listener nods their head in regular intervals.

Hands and arms say a lot. It's never a good idea to cross your arms, if at all possible. It's habitual for a lot of us to cross our arms when we're cold, or we just don't know what to do with them. But when a person has a nervous, negative or defensive attitude, it is likely they'll fold their arms on their chest, displaying that they feel threatened. Crossed arms on the chest are universally perceived as defensive or negative. You might not feel negative, nervous or defensive, but, if your arms are crossed, it's how you are perceived. Also, avoid crossing your feet, which can be seen as negative too.

The hands have been the most important tools in human evolution. There are more connections between the brain and the hands than any other part of the body. With your hands, be expressive, but don't overdo it. Keep your fingers closed when you gesture, and keep your hands below your chin level. As for personal safety, watch the hands, because whatever is in the hands can injure you—or even worse. We'll cover that more in Chapter 5.

Throughout history, the open palm has been associated with truth, honesty, allegiance and submission. Hiding your palms—when you put your hands behind your back—gives a person an intuitive feeling that you're not telling the truth. So keep your hands out in front of you.

If you want to appear non-threatening, have your palms up. In ancient times, you would expose your palms when approaching the gate, the kingdom, the castle to show that you had no weapons.

Palms down show authority or assertiveness. It's the way to say "calm down" without saying it verbally. Palms up and out towards another person, either one or both palms, is the universal sign for "stop."

Be aware of your stance. Remember to use the 45-degree angle versus facing people face-to-face or head-on, which is potentially confrontational. When you slightly angle your body, it demonstrates that you're non-threatening.

All of your non-verbal communication, whether it's being communicated from your face, your eye contact, your body language, your postures, gestures, hands, or even your stance expresses, the most important part of your communication—that you are non-threatening, that you are friendly.

Cultural differences are important to note. They exist mainly in relation to territorial space (distance from another person), amount of eye contact, touching and insult gestures. If you're communicating with people from Arab countries, parts of Asia or Japan, become familiar with their customs. Those regions have the most differences in gestures and body language.

Keep Your Distance

"Spatial empathy" is an informal term used to describe the awareness of an individual to the proximity, activities and comfort of people around them. What is the first thing you do when you get on an elevator? You put your back against the wall. The reason you protect your back side is because you can't see behind yourself. When I go to a restaurant with my family, my family already knows where I'm going to sit; I like to keep my back against the wall. I'm not paranoid or scared, I just want to see who comes in and out of the restaurant. When I can see the exits, I can protect my family's backside.

Having spatial empathy means that you're aware of your personal zones and the personal zones of other people around you. One person's presence and/or proximity can affect another person's comfort or discomfort. There are several factors that affect a person's comfort or spacial empathy:

- Gender. Men are more territorial than women. Men like their space.

- Culture. In some cultures, making body contact is appropriate; in others it's not.

- Environment. People's distancing around one another depends on the environment you're in. In a crowded bar, shoulder to shoulder is expected; at a business meeting, that would be inappropriate.

- Upbringing. Were you raised in a hugging, affectionate family, or a family that was very hands-off? That kind of thing helps determine how close you want other people to you.

- Past experiences. Has somebody ever gotten in your face and tried to intimidate you? That can make you a lot less tolerant of people invading your space.

There's a physiological and a psychological response when people invade your personal zone, what I call space invaders. If a person invades your personal zone your safety is compromised. In Chapter 7, you'll learn about time and distance, and how to keep yourself safe with both.

Do People Just Snap?

I've asked that question in classes for a number of years, "Do people just snap?" I ask for a show of hands, and I'll get people to raise their hands and say, yes they do—and I'll get people who say no. I tell my audience, they're both right.

Sometimes, depending on what you do for an occupation, you might have to respond to a situation where it appears that a person has just snapped. But you were just not there to see the signs of escalation. There are always signs and symptoms that a person is escalating. Always.

I call it the Assault Cycle. People start with stress, sometimes intoxication, go from stress to being angry, and from angry to being combative. Escalation doesn't always happen in that order, though, and drugs or alcohol can influence the Assault Cycle. It's important to use the appropriate intervention skills depending on what level of the cycle you're dealing with.

Again, the Assault Cycle includes individuals who are stressed, intoxicated, angry and combative. Caution should be used when dealing with any of these behaviors. The following information will help you recognize the signs and symptoms of the behaviors in the Assault Cycle, as well as give you verbal and non-verbal personal safety intervention techniques to deal with these behaviors.

We've all been stressed. Most of us have dealt with people who were stressed. There are many signs and symptoms of stress. I'm going to touch on a few, and I want you to think about additional signs and symptoms of individuals who are stressed.

We all have these little nervous tics. Poker players call it a tell. Some people tap, fidget, bounce their knee, shake their feet, twirl their hair, play with their glasses, chain smoke, whatever it may be. Everybody has a tell, a little nervous tic, twitch or habit that shows they are stressed about something.

- Skin Color: Under stress, a person's face changes in color, blushing, turning red.
- Eye Contact: When some people are stressed, they maintain less eye contact with another person. However, some people will maintain more eye contact when they're stressed.
- Facial Changes: Stress causes changes in facial expression.
- Changes in Speech: People will stutter. They'll repeat their phrases. Their speech fluency changes, they'll hesitate more.
- Fidgeting: People can't sit calmly and still. They'll fidget with their clothes, items on their desk, things in their hands, whatever—just continually move things around.

If you're stressed, it means you're distracted. You're thinking about what could happen or what did happen, past or future. People are confused when they're stressed because they're not in the present. You can go to any waiting room in the country and see people pacing nervously around because of the stress they're experiencing, what they're expecting to hear or to find out. The key to avoiding stress and anxiety is to live in the moment.

Staying Safe When You See Escalation

There are several safety interventions for dealing with stressed individuals. These guidelines will keep you safe.

Rule #1: Control your behavior. Remember the equation from earlier? Incident plus response equals outcome ($I + R = O$). So if I'm dealing with a person who's stressed, that's an *incident*. My *response* to them is going to determine the *outcome*. So if I can control my own behavior, my body language, my words and the manner in which I speak them, that is how I control my behavior. Use a calm voice with people who are stressed.

You're taught that in first aid training: you don't scream, "Oh, my Goodness!" You're calm and reassuring in your words and in your tone.

Rule #2: Assess your own body language. Make sure that you're using the appropriate body language during this intervention of dealing with stressed people.

Rule #3: Trust your intuition. What's your intuition telling you about this? Listen to that. Listen to those inner signals that give you that valuable insight into a person who is stressed and what you should do.

Rule #4: Assess the area and the space around you and the person.

What's in that area that can be used against you? How far away are you from the stressed individual? Allow enough time to respond should things escalate. Give yourself at least arm's length and a little more distance from the stressed individual.

Rule #5: If you can, redirect a person's thoughts and/or their environment. If you can get a person to think about something else, change the subject, talk about something different, talk about yourself. Make up a story to redirect them. Change the environment by asking a person to move, "Walk with me," "Let's go out here and talk about this," "Let's go get a cup of coffee." Get them out of the environment that they're in.

Remember, we've all been stressed and you have all dealt with stressed individuals. So the signs and symptoms are pretty common, and the intervention skills are pretty straightforward.

"Raise your hand if you've never been angry," I ask that to people all the time. You know how many hands I see? Zero. We've all been angry, angry at the situation, another person, ourselves. But not all of us escalate. Not everyone goes from being angry to being combative. Most of us have coping skills to deal with anger.

Some people don't have coping skills, though, and they do escalate. Always be cautious in dealing with people who are angry.

You Know They're Angry When...

The signs and symptoms of anger are pretty straightforward.

Louder and More Offensive: When people are angry, they get louder, they start to vocalize what they're angry about. They often lash out with foul language, obscenities, sometimes directed at you, or other people, or the situation.

Verbally Threatening: Verbal threats are common with people who are angry. They'll threaten the situation, they'll threaten you, other people.

Exaggerated Body Language: They might stomp their feet, pound their fist on the table, kick or hit the wall. But remember, it doesn't necessarily mean that they're going to be combative against you. This person is just acting out their frustration and anger. It could happen, but it doesn't necessarily mean that it's going to happen.

Personal History: If you have information about a person's history, if they're a family member or somebody you know, a client, or a patient, that gives you additional insight as to whether or not this person will escalate more, deescalate, or just stay angry. And, obviously, using that history and previous interventions will help as well.

Demanding Expressions: When people are angry, their expressions get demanding. That finger comes out, the eyebrows start to drop.

You can sense aggression in people. Not only can you sense it, but you can see it, and you can feel it. So how do you deal with people who are angry? If you can, *walk away*. Avoid people who are angry, if you can. All the interventions that we talked about for stress can also be used for dealing with people who are angry, but walking away is your best choice. If you can't walk away, here are some coping tactics:

Seek to agree with a person who is angry. This is a customer service skill that I teach. If you can get a person to agree, you can get them to comply, you can get them to go with the program, to de-escalate themselves. So agree with them. Don't interrupt, let them vent. I know when I feel angry and I vent, share my feelings with people whom I trust, I feel a lot better. I feel a lot better about getting that off my chest, getting that out of me. So don't interrupt, even if the person is getting irrational or being unfair. Let the person get it out.

Offer options. "I hear that you're upset about this. Here's what we can do, [option1] or [option2]." You're redirecting and offering solutions.

Identify the problem. More than likely, YOU are not the problem. You're just the handiest person for an angry person to vent to. But if you can help the individual identify the problem, it can redirect their anger away from you.

Use a collaborative approach. Use the following types of statements with "we" or "us": "Maybe we need to look at this a different way," "Why don't we get a cup of coffee and sit down," "Let's try to figure this out together." It's an association that you're in it together, that you're part of a group or a team to intervene with the particular situation.

Set and enforce boundaries, if you need to. Some people will vent and vent and vent and vent and vent, and they'll work themselves up. You might have to put the brakes on, and set some limits and say no, this is it. When you set those limits and boundaries, you've got to enforce them. With people who are angry or escalating, you have to stay in control of the situation.

Express your feelings. When someone is making you uncomfortable because of their behavior, tell them. "You're scaring me," or "I'm upset about how you're behaving towards me." Letting them know that you have feelings as well and that you're frightened by what they're doing.

Assess the area and the space around you. Do you know, what can be used against you in this area? How close are you to this individual? These are things we talked about earlier. So be aware of that.

He's fine when he's sober, but he's a mean drunk.

Always be cautious when dealing with people who are under the influence of alcohol, drugs, or even prescribed drugs. Know the signs and symptoms of intoxication—and remember that the Assault Cycle doesn't always apply. Someone under the influence of alcohol or drugs can escalate quickly.

So what are the signs that someone is not sober?

Slurred Speech: When a person is intoxicated, their speech becomes slurred. Sometimes people talk faster, sometimes they'll talk slower, but you can hear the slur in their speech a lot of times.

Unsteady: A person's balance is compromised when they're under the influence. Their equilibrium is affected. Stumbling, swaying, falling down, leaning against walls or furniture to stay upright are all signs that something is wrong.

Eyes: When a person is high or drunk, their eyes will send that message. On speed, a person's eyes are wide open, sometimes too wide. The pupils literally look bigger. On alcohol or downers, the eyes look smaller; eyelids may be at "half-mast." Look at their eyes. Are they glossy? Are the pupils getting big? Are they getting small? You want to be aware of that.

Change in Attitude: Under the influence, people are up, they're down. They can become very emotional, and have fast, violent mood swings. Be aware of those signs.

Odors: Can you smell alcohol on a person? Do you know the pungent smell of marijuana? Sometimes a sour body odor, in conjunction with the other warning signs, can also be a hint.

Arguing: People get argumentative when they've been drinking or using drugs. They want to argue their point that they're right, no matter how irrational or unimportant. Agreeing with this kind of person is particularly helpful.

Loud AND Obnoxious: Most bouncers, bartenders, and people who work in nightclubs will tell you that when you add alcohol, the place gets louder. People get obnoxious, too. Loud, slurred speech will tell you you're dealing with a drunk, but not necessarily an *angry* drunk. So look for all the other signals.

Obviously, you must always use caution in dealing with people who are under the influence. Stay aware. Be aware of your environment, your space around others and what people are doing. Don't argue with a person who's under the influence. Let them be right, seek to agree with them. Let them win the argument, so to speak.

But, also be proactive. Being proactive means that you *avoid these situations* in the first place. If I can get up and walk out of the bar, the nightclub, party, wherever I am dealing with this person or persons under the influence, and just avoid it, I am being proactive in my response. My training partner told me this story recently:

> I was at a barbecue, and one guy was really drunk. He knew I was a retired cop, and after he'd had too many, he started trying to verbally assault me. Honestly, I don't even remember what he said; he was just giving me crap about being a cop. He was drunk, he was stupid, and he was escalating. But I was his target, and I knew

without that target, he'd calm down. I knew the best way
to de-escalate the situation was to remove his target. So I
got up and left.

Some people might think, "Why should I leave? I have as much right
to be here as the drunk guy!" That's true—but is it worth it? It is worth
risking your safety—or anyone else's—to prove a point? My training partner is a tough guy. He has a black belt in Karate, and he has nothing to
prove. He wanted to make sure no one got hurt, and the best way to ensure
that was by walking away.

Use all the intervention skills that we talked about for stress and anger.
Those will also work for people who are under the influence. But remember, people can be unpredictable and it can escalate quickly when someone
is under the influence of drugs and alcohol.

I just wanted to get out of there

What frightens us the most is dealing with a combative person. In a
combative situation, ESCAPE!! As soon as you recognize the danger, get
out of there. Don't second-guess yourself, don't worry about explaining
yourself to anyone, just get out of there. I have more than thirty years of
martial arts experience, I was a successful full-contact fighter, but my first
instinct is always to get away.

I've worked with thousands of police officers, security officers, and
emergency department personnel over the years, and I've asked them
questions about dealing with combative individuals. I always ask, "Do you
sense, feel or have the ability to see when a person is going to become
combative?" Most of them will say yes, that there are indicators, signs and
symptoms that a person is escalating to violence. What are the signs and
symptoms of a person that is getting combative?

Change in posture. The person tightens up. When a person is in the
fight/flight response, the blood leaves the extremities and goes to the core,
the torso, and you start to see that person tense up, getting ready to fight.

The face goes pale. Angry people have red faces; violent people have
pale faces. The blood leaves all the extremities, including the head. You
can see the whites of the knuckles because the blood is going to the core.

Facial expression can also change due to this vasoconstriction process, similar to a person that is going through a shock process.

Changes in verbalization. In my experience in dealing with combative individuals on the street, in the health care environment, in ERs and psychiatric units, I've noticed that men and women do one thing very differently. When a male is going into the combative stage, he'll stop verbalizing. He'll stop talking and communicating. But female aggressors usually increase their verbalization, talking, yelling, screaming. People always laugh when I tell them that in trainings, but the difference, I *think*, is in our ability to multitask. Men are uni-taskers; when we're going to fight, we stop talking. Women are more apt to be multi-taskers; they can fight and verbalize at the same time.

Telegraphing intentions. Pick up a pen. Go ahead, pick one up. What did you do immediately before picking it up? You looked at it.

People telegraph with their eyes. You look down at this book, you're telegraphing your intentions as you read the pages. As you reach out to pick up that glass in front of you, you telegraph with your eyes. If someone is about to strike you, he will look at the place he's going to strike. If someone is about to use a lamp to clock you on the head, she'll look at the lamp. Watch where the aggressor's eyes go, it will tell you what his next step is.

Exaggerated movements. If you make a fist right now, with the intention to slam it down on the table, first of all, you'll brace yourself. You'll tighten your fist, maybe you're whole body, before you hit the desk. That kind of tensing is an exaggerated movement that clues you in to a possible violent attack. An aggressor will also puff up his shoulders and push them back, bracing themselves before they strike.

Distraction. "Look over there!" It's the oldest trick in the book, and for good reason. It works. Before an aggressor tries to hit you, they might try to get you to look away so they can get in a "sucker punch". Be aware of obvious distraction attempts.

Escape, Escape, Escape

When you see signs of imminent violence, escape, escape, escape. Is that clear enough? Get AWAY! But if escape is not an immediate option, use your defensive presence, then get away.

Loud yells and screams distract a combatant individual. So get loud, scream, yell "No!" or "Stop!" as loud as you can. Stay at that heightened level of awareness. Avoid tunnel vision. There might be other threats and other things that you need to be aware of.

Use distractions. Put your hand out, a person will look at that. That distracts their eyes. Look behind them. They might turn around to see what you're looking at, which can give you time to escape. If you're in a work area that has panic alarms, or if you can key your phone somehow to alert others, do whatever you can to alert others to get you help. Try to alert others by motioning and verbalizing. Don't get sucked into this conflict. Use all of your defensive intervention skills, and only use physical self-defense as a last resort if escape is not possible.

If you can't get away, bring your hands up in a bladed position, with your body bladed away from the aggressor to protect your vulnerable line. We'll go into more about self-defense in Chapter 5, but those basics will keep you safe until you can get away.

I told you earlier that my goal in this book is for you to never even be in a situation where you're unsafe. How can you use your interpersonal communication skills to keep yourself safe? There are some simple things you can do to help.

You've heard of the Golden Rule—do unto others as you would have them do unto you. The Platinum Rule says to treat others the way they want to be treated. Treating and speaking to people with respect is universally accepted, right? So use common courtesies: "please," "thank you," "yes, please," "my pleasure," "you're welcome," "I'm sorry to disturb you." Use them consistently and repeatedly with all people.

Be clear and concise in your communication. Avoid using slang and jargon when speaking to people. This helps avoid confusion, misdirection, complaints and poor interpersonal relationships.

People-watch and pay attention. This is huge. Watch and learn. Pay attention to what works and what doesn't work. Practice the skills you learned in this chapter, and of course, learn from your experience and the experience of others. Experience is the greatest teacher.

"I've always said, I believe self-defense is our God-given right."

-David Fowler

Chapter 5

Legal Defense of Self and Others

D o you have the right to defend yourself? Can you get into legal trouble by defending yourself? Can a person who has attacked you file assault charges against you if you injure them defending yourself? Is self-defense a right, or is it a last resort? Do you know your rights—what is reasonable when it comes to defending yourself or defending another person? Those are all important questions.

In this chapter, you'll get a broad understanding of what self-defense is, what you can do legally, what you can't do legally, how to protect yourself from a physical attack, and how do you protect yourself legally.[6]

What is self-defense? For the purposes of this chapter and this book, it is defined as: "The right to use reasonable force to protect one's self or members of one's family—and even, to a lesser extent, one's property—from bodily harm due to the attack of an aggressor, if you have reason to believe that you are in danger." That, of course, leads to the question, what is "reasonable force?" It's defined as: "the degree of force which is not excessive and is appropriate in protecting oneself or one's property."

I believe self-defense is a God-given right. Your ability and your right

---

[6] **Important Legal Disclaimer:** In no way can we dictate policies or procedures for the use of any self-defense or any physical intervention for use by a department/agency or private individual. The suggestions/ options disseminated in this book are simply that, suggestions or options. Each individual, department or agency is responsible for developing their own "policies and procedures" regarding the use of self-defense and physical intervention for their personnel or for themselves.

to defend yourself is a freedom that we're fortunate to have. If somebody tries to stop you from doing something or physically grabs you or holds you, you have the right to defend yourself against that, and the law will stand behind you, as long as you use "reasonable force" (which we will discuss more in-depth later in this chapter). Force should be your last resort; if you can get away safely and call the police, do it. But if you're in a situation where you can't get away, you can't escape, you do have the legal right to physically defend yourself against what you believe to be imminent danger.

Of course, you will have to take into consideration your own ability, any policies and procedures of your employer (if you're defending yourself while at work), and the laws in the state and country.

What Is "Assault"?

There are four types of assault: physical assault, non-physical assault, battery, and domestic assault. Depending on where you live, what state or country you reside in, there might be different names or categories for these assault types, but these are general.

Physical Assault: Any attempt to threaten or attack another party.

Non-Physical Assault: An attempt to assault another party, but physical contact is not needed to constitute a non-physical assault.

Battery Assault: Battery is a criminal offense whereby one party makes physical contact with another with the intention to harm them. In order to constitute a battery, an offense must be intentional and must be committed to inflict injury on another person. Sexual battery is defined as any non-consensual physical contact that is sexual in nature.

Domestic Assault: Can involve battery. Occurs between two parties who are related by some degree, family (siblings, parents, relatives) or an intimate relationship (spouses, boyfriends, girlfriends, live-in or live-out partners).

What Can You Do to Defend Yourself?

When it comes to your physical actions in defending yourself, you very well might be held accountable for what you do. So it's important to understand some legal definitions when it comes to a lawful use of de fense. In order to be lawful in your defense of yourself and others, we must have a basic understanding of these legal definitions and how they apply to self-defense and the legal system. Let's define them first, then go into more detail to understand each one.

Reasonable Force: Reasonable force is defined as the degree of force which is not excessive and is appropriate in protecting oneself or one's property. When such force is used, a person is justified and is not criminally liable nor is he liable in tort. ("Tort" is an act that injures someone in some way, and for which the injured person may sue the wrongdoer for damages.) So, for lawful, reasonable self-defense, you should not be liable in tort. It's pretty important to understand.

Reasonable Belief: When you use self-defense, what you believe must also be reasonable, believe it or not.

Deadly Force: Any use of force that is likely or intended to cause death or great bodily harm. It may be reasonable or unreasonable depending on the circumstances.

Excessive Force: The amount of force which is beyond the need and circumstances of a particular event, or which is not justified in light of all the circumstances.

Dangerous Weapons: Any firearm, whether it's loaded or unloaded. Always assume that any firearm, regardless of what you know about it, is a dangerous weapon. Any device which is designed as a weapon and capable of producing death or great bodily harm is also considered a dangerous weapon. So the obvious are knives, machetes and hatchets, swords, throwing stars, etc.

Deadly Weapons: Any firearms or other weapons, devices, instruments, materials or substances, whether animate or inanimate, which in the manner they are used or intended to be used are known to be capable of producing death or serious bodily injury. The obvious are guns, knives, and different types of poisons.

How All That Applies in the Real World

Reasonable Force

If I get up in your face and start calling you a "no good son of a bitch," would you have the right, or would it be reasonable for you, to strike me in the face? It's a pretty obvious one, isn't it? No, that wouldn't be reasonable force. However, might there be some other circumstances around that—if I'm in your way, not allowing you to get away, and calling you a name? Well, you might be justified in using some type of physical defense to get away. But if you struck someone because he was just calling you a name, it would not be reasonable, and you will be held liable. You could get arrested and go to jail.

If I grab onto you and hold you, would it be reasonable for you to do some type of self-defense intervention? More than likely, yes. We'd have to look at all the facts, all the circumstances, generally, if someone touches you to restrain you, you can use a reasonable self-defense technique to get away.

Generally, the court system will look at a situation that you're being held liable for, and ask, would another person have done the same thing, based on the circumstances known to them at the time the situation took place? If it's deemed that a reasonable person would have done the same type of defense or control based on the circumstances known to them, then that would determine what reasonable force is.

But what is reasonable for you might be not reasonable for me.

A hundred-pound, untrained woman would almost certainly be deemed reasonable if she hit, kicked, or punched a man who was restraining her. I have two black belts in martial arts, experience as a full-contact fighter, and extensive training in defensive tactics. If a man grabbed my arm, "reasonable force" would probably mean that I used a defensive move to get away, not that I knock him unconscious.

Reasonable Belief

In the same example—someone grabs your arm—did you reasonably believe that this person was not going to let you go? Did you reasonably believe that this person was going to hurt you, was going to assault you, was going to commit battery against you? Are you reasonable in your belief of this? Would another person have done the same thing that you've done based on what they knew, based on the context of the situation? If so, that's reasonable force based on reasonable belief. You will have to justify your beliefs— that you believed this person was going to hurt you, that he was not going to let you go, that he was going to assault you.

Can you be preemptive in using a self-defense technique, or even a defensive strike against a person before they grab you? Again, if you believe that they are going to hurt you, going to harm you, imminent danger is present, you might be reasonable in applying force against the person based on your beliefs about the person and the situation.

Deadly Force

If somebody was holding a knife to your throat, or had a gun in your face, that is clearly a threat of deadly force being used against you. Would it be reasonable to strike that person in the throat, to strike them in the eyes, causing serious injury to that person, so that you could get away? Would your force against them be reasonable? Yes, it would. If your life is threatened, you would be justified and reasonable to use force against that force that is being used against you. In other words, are you lawful in upping the ante? Yes. Based on the circumstances that you know at that time, if this is deadly force being used against you, you can use deadly force against that person to survive, to win, to go home. Ultimately, that's your lawful right. That is your God-given right to defend yourself.

Excessive Force

This seems like a straight-forward concept: for example, if a person gets in your face and says that they don't like you and that you're an idiot, and you hit them over the head with a chair and caused them serious injury, that would be excessive force. But it can be more convoluted than that.

We hear the term "excessive force" mostly in regards to law enforcement, because officers can be held liable for using excessive force. Officers can be cited—or even sued—for using excessive force if the officers did more than was needed to control the subject or the situation.

But as civilians, any of us could be held accountable in using excessive force. We could get arrested. We could be criminally charged for using excessive force. So it's important to understand, it has to be reasonable. You have to have reasonable belief in what you do.

Can you use deadly force to protect property? If you're a security officer or a protection officer working with critical infrastructure, a nuclear power plant, you know, those types of institutions have threats of terrorism. They would be lawful in using deadly force to protect that critical infrastructure. But for the most part, us as civilians, we would not be lawful in using deadly force to protect property. So in other words, if somebody jumps in your car and takes off with it and you shoot them and kill them, there's a very good chance that you could be criminally charged for that.

Again, I can't make a legal statement or recommendation for using force. I am just giving you a basic understanding of legal definitions, and what is appropriate and reasonable in regards to using force to protect yourself or another person.

Dangerous Weapons and Deadly Weapons

When you see a gun, you assume it's loaded, right? The replicas they make these days, the airsoft guns, are very realistic. If you lay one of those next to a real firearm, it's very difficult to tell the difference. Always assume that any firearm you see is a dangerous weapon.

Any device which is designed as a weapon and capable of producing death or great bodily harm is also considered a dangerous weapon. Again, the obvious are guns, knives, machetes, hatchets, swords, throwing stars, etc. But if I pick up a screwdriver and jam it into a person's torso, that's a dangerous weapon, too. I'm using a generally harmless tool to inflict harm. If the manner in which it is used is likely to produce death or great bodily harm, the screwdriver became a dangerous or even deadly weapon.

Look in your environment right now. Look around. Do a scan. What in your environment right now can be used against you as a dangerous weapon? I ask this question all the time when I'm working with emergency room personnel, nurses, and security officers in the health care industry: What in your environment can be used against you to cause you serious injury and even death?

The first to come up is always pens. Where do you carry pens? Right in your pocket. They're readily available. A pen could be shoved into your body, stuck in your eye. What about the name badge holder you wear around your neck? It could be used to strangle you. Anything that can be picked up and thrown at another person would be considered a dangerous weapon: keyboards, computers, chairs, TVs, anything. Everyday common tools, devices or instruments can be used as dangerous or even deadly weapons. A dangerous weapon can easily turn into a deadly weapon. Again, it's about having that awareness. Know your environment.

Civilian Levels of Defense

Police, military and security personnel are required to follow certain rules of engagement. This chart below shows *civilian* levels of defense, and is designed to give you an understanding of how to use defense in a lawful manner.

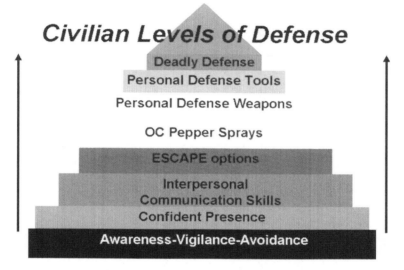

This whole pyramid stands on the base of awareness, vigilance and avoidance. Now you know that your best defense is to be aware, be vigilant, and avoid conflicts if at all possible.

Up one level from Awareness, Vigilance and Avoidance is a confident presence. A confident presence is a major deterrent against predators. Have a confident posture and facial expression, and use eye communication to show that you are not an easy target.

The third level is interpersonal communication skills. When faced with people who are stressed, angry, intoxicated or combative, your best initial defense is your ability to communicate, to de-escalate with your words and your body language.

Next is escape. When faced with a situation that is escalating and dangerous, if possible, escape to a safe location and alert others.

If escape is not possible, go up one level to using pepper spray as a defense. Pepper spray is a non-lethal force option which can distract a predator, giving you time to escape or time to defend. Ground pepper has been used as a defense for thousands of years. In fact, Samurai warriors would blow it into opponents' eyes to impede their ability to see and fight.

Above this non-lethal force option are your personal defensive weapons. Your personal defensive weapons are your body, your hands, your feet, your ability to use escape techniques. An elbow strike, a palm heel strike, a knee strike, a foot stomp, a head butt—those are all personal defensive weapons.

Personal defense tools are an extension of your hands, that's why I call them tools versus weapons. These are any non-deadly items which you can use in your hands to defend yourself. Examples are key chains, umbrellas, flashlights, rolled up newspapers, etc.

At the peak, at the top of your pyramid of the civilian levels of self-defense, is deadly defense. If you believe you are facing serious injury or death at the hands of someone, would you be justified in using deadly defense against that person? Again, you must take into consideration your legal rights, and moral and ethical beliefs when using any type of force to defend yourself or others.

Tiger Mindset

I have a favorite Chinese proverb: "Better to be a tiger for a day than a sheep for a lifetime." When I think about this Chinese proverb, it reminds me that I might face a situation that brings that tiger out of me. If I need to, if my life is threatened, I will take the attitude that I'm going to win, I'm going to survive, I'm going to go home. That attitude, that tiger mindset, will get me through the situation. I'm not going to be a sheep; I won't give up, give in, submit, or surrender. I will not be a victim.

This tiger mindset is hard for some people to develop, or even think about. The dangerous victim/prey mentality is, "that will never happen to me." And I'm not saying it will happen to you; what I'm saying is that you can build your mental awareness, that mental attitude so that if something does happen, you will respond the way the tiger responds. That's a shift from "it'll never happen to me," to "I will never ALLOW that to happen to me."

Maybe you're still having a hard time thinking of yourself as a tiger. But think about your cubs—your kids. Do you want to get home to them? Do you want to be around to see them live a safe and productive life? Maybe that's the attitude that you have to develop, you have to adopt in regards to having that tiger mindset. It's all up to you. It always has been. Personal safety and self-defense is your responsibility, no one else's.

Tigers Will Do ANYTHING to Get Away

We've all heard stories about animals gnawing off a limb to get out of trap. That's extreme. But are you willing to get hurt—to be physically hurt, cut, injured, bruised, whatever—in your defense against yourself or another person? Are you willing to do that? Will you sacrifice getting injured to prevent something worse? Would you take a bad cut or broken bone to prevent yourself from getting raped, getting injured, or possibly being killed?

That's the attitude you have to develop. It starts right now, when you're safe, in this mindset you train yourself for—not in the middle of a dangerous situation. When it happens then, you don't have time to think about it and stress is going to distract your mind as well.

Right now is the time to decide that you will have that tiger mindset: that you're not going to be a victim, that you're going to do whatever it takes to escape, to defend yourself, to get back home to your family and your friends. You decide right now.

Report... and CYA

People will sue for just about anything. People sue for hot coffee spilled in their lap. You can't really stop a person from filing some type of suit against you. It could be frivolous, but that's why this whole chapter on defense of self and others is so important, so that you can be lawful in your actions when it comes to defending yourself.

When it comes to defending yourself, you're going to do what's needed when you take action. But after the fact, you'll want to report it. Start the documentation immediately. Contact your local law enforcement agency and file a report immediately. If it happens at your work place, file a report with your security department. Start that paper trail—who, what, where, when, why and how.

When it comes to documenting, the more explicit, the more detailed you are, the better off you're going to be. Report—and record—what happened before the incident, what happened during the incident, and then of course what happened after the incident. You have to document and report your actions when using physical levels of defense. You just have to, to protect yourself. You need to be very clear about what happened, and why you did what you did to defend yourself.

Also, it's healthy to get it down on paper so that you can help de-escalate yourself, so that you can get that out of you. Any situation where you are required to defend yourself is stressful at the least, and probably traumatic. Have you ever been really angry at another person, and you wrote that person a letter? You got it all out. Didn't you feel better? I know I did. Any counselor or therapist will tell you that the healthiest thing you can do for yourself is talk about any traumatic incident.

When you're documenting, think about what you learned in Chapter 3 on avoidance. Think about the signals that the predator sent you; it's going to help you in your justification of your defense. As that person clenched her fist, she looked at you. You could sense in her eyes that she was staring through you, that you were going to be the target of her attack as she got close to you. Those are details that you can document that will justify your level of self-defense. What the predator said—did he threaten you? Put that in quotation marks, as close as you can get to exactly what he said. Were there witnesses? Get their names and contact information, so that if this goes further, and you have to justify your actions, you've got witnesses.

I teach security officers report writing skills for their incident documentation. I tell them, if you fight, you write, and the longer you fight, the more you write. You have to document *everything*—it's absolutely critical. Because what do people sue for? Anything and everything. Remember the old saying: "CYA—Cover your assets." So, literally cover your assets. Protect yourself.

"It's not stress that kills us, it's our reaction to it."

-Hans Selye

Chapter 6

Manage Your Stress
So You Can AVADE® Danger

In 1975, Hans Selye, a Doctor of Medicine and Chemistry, developed a model on stress where he divided it into two categories. He labeled persistent stress, which is not resolved by a coping mechanism or adaptation, as "distress." Distress leads to anxiety, withdrawal and depression.

Activities that enhance your physical or mental functions—and that you enjoy—create "eustress." Strength training is a good example; it puts stress on your muscles, but makes them stronger and better. (If you don't enjoy strength training, though, and you force yourself to do it, it creates distress, too.) Challenging work is another good example. When you love your job, challenging projects may cause you stress, but you love the challenge of getting the job done. The difference between eustress and distress is just how you look at it.

We all have distress and eustress in our lives. For me personally, when I'm worried about a situation, I feel a threat or a danger, it becomes distressful to me. But when I'm working out, I'm running, I'm training, I'm preparing myself, I'm working on a project, I'm writing this book, that's eustress. It still puts some tension on me, but it's positive tension that I need. It takes me forward and allows me to grow.

Fight or Flight

Facing a fight-or-flight situation could be considered both eustress and distress. It just all depends on how you cope with it, how you deal with it, and how your body and mind are prepared to deal with the conflict.

The fight-or-flight response is a primal, physiological urge to defend or flee in times of danger. You don't have to face down tigers in the wild anymore, but you have probably faced some situation where that primal instinct kicked in. "Janine" told me this story:

> Back in high school, twenty-some years ago, I was on a football field and some girls—the "mean girls" in my school—approached me and surrounded me. I felt very threatened, that they were going to physically harm me. I guess I went into that fight-or-flight response, but my response was to flee! I ran so fast, I have never experienced that ability of running that fast ever again in my life.

When faced with a situation that is frightening, your perception of it stimulates the part of the brain called the hypothalamus. The hypothalamus emits a hormone that stimulates the pituitary gland to release substances that excite the adrenal gland to release adrenalin, epinephrine and cortisol. This chemical response gives you strength. It gives you speed. It gives you that ability to do what you need to do beyond what you're normally capable of. We've all heard accounts of the little lady who managed to lift a vehicle off her husband after the jack fell and trapped him under it. In normal circumstances, this woman would never be able to lift the 2,000-plus-pound vehicle off of anybody. But the magic of adrenaline gave her that super strength.

Adrenalin stimulates the heart to beat faster, and certain blood vessels to open wider, pushing more blood to your muscles. The vessels that run the digestive and the eliminative organs constrict, blood pressure goes up and more blood is being pumped, but many vessels constrict to slow the blood flow. Breath becomes faster and shallower or you might even hold your breath during a fight-or-flight situation. Blood shunts systematically from the organs to the muscles, preparing you to fight or to take flight. It is instinctual. It's primal. This is part of your ability that evolved to help you to get away from the saber-tooth tiger, the bear, that danger, that threat, so that you could survive. If it wasn't for the fight-or-flight, humanity would not have evolved; we would not have developed the ability to adapt and overcome and to be here today.

What's the worst thing that you can do when danger is ever present? Freeze up, stand there, do nothing. The fight-or-flight can save you.

It's All in How You Frame It

How do you respond to a stressful situation? Do you throw your hands up in despair? Do you get angry? Do you withdraw and become depressed? Or do you get energized? It probably depends on the situation. What type of stress are you experiencing?

The fight-or-flight may seem like a distressful situation, but really, it's eustress. If you prepare and train and plan for stressful events, you're likely to fall back into an automatic response. Again, it's about forming habits that promote your own safety. You can train yourself so that when you're stressed, you automatically respond a certain way. Erin told me another story:

> It's been drilled into me to breathe away stress. Now, whenever I find myself stressed about a deadline, or a bill, or my kids, the first thing I do, as soon as I realize I'm stressed, is take a few deep breaths. It's finally spilling over to physical stress, too. The other day, a broom fell over in my kitchen. I swear, it was so loud it sounded like a gun shot. I literally jumped—talk about jumping out of your skin. As soon as I realized what had made the noise, I took a deep breath—without even thinking about it. Before, my heart would have been pounding, and I would have gotten a headache from it a few minutes later. In fact, I used to think there was something wrong with me, because I always got a headache a few minutes after a loud noise startled me. Now I realize it's part of my stress response, and I can breathe it away!

The Breath of Life

Studies have shown that during the process of slow, deep breathing, endorphins are released causing a feeling of general well-being and relaxation. Breathing correctly is an automatic stress reducer. Consciously-controlled breathing is a very useful tactic in lowering your blood pressure, and the endorphins apply a break to the hypothalamic fight-or-flight response in a situation of imminent danger. So you can put the brakes on immediately by using proper breath.

Conscious-controlled breathing and conscious positive thinking are considered the best stress management techniques for immediate stressors, or just everyday life. Right now, inhale slowly about two-thirds of your lung capacity. Take that big, deep breath and bring your diaphragm out. Breathe in for a count of four seconds, hold for one second, then breathe out slowly for a count of eight seconds. Again, expand your diaphragm, breathe in for a count of four, hold for one second, and exhale for a count of eight. You're doubling the length of exhalations. You're really getting that old stagnant air out of you and revitalizing your body with new, fresh air. Practice that a few times right now.

An old Chinese proverb states that if you master breath, you will have the strength of ten tigers. We, as Westerners, give very little thought to our breath. Most of us don't breathe into our diaphragms, we breathe only into our upper chests. But watch a baby breathe. Their tummies go up, and then down—they're naturally diaphragmic breathers. But as you got older, you stopped diaphragmic breathing, you started to breathe thoraxically, in your upper chest, which doesn't give you that full life experience. (Personally, I think it's thanks to our society telling us to "suck it in.") When you don't get rid of that stagnated oxygen, you don't increase those endorphins and that overall feeling of well-being and your ability to reduce your stress.

If I know I have to walk into a difficult or threatening situation, I consciously prepare myself by doing some deep breathing. As a full contact fighter, one of the things I mastered was the ability to inhale and exhale consciously. I knew that if I wasn't focused on my breathing, I would tax my energy and I would distract my mind. Breath is the key.

You Are What You *Think*

In Feudal Japan, Samurai spent as much time in mental training as they did in preparing their bodies for battle. Using breath control and meditation, Samurai prepared their minds to be tranquil, fearless and energetic in combat. Meditation clears the mind and prepares it for combat, training, or just overall life. The Samurai knew that a warrior filled with fear and negative thoughts was doomed. Fear inhibits the ability to think quickly or to act fully. Conscious positive thinking programs the brain—we're back to those mental movies again.

Remember the Little Engine That Could? It said, "I think I can. I think I can. I think I can." That's positive conscious thinking. If that little train had said, "I don't think I can make it," the little engine would never have made it over the mountain, and it wouldn't be a famous children's book.

You are what you think—period. To change your life, you change your thoughts. If you're facing some stressful, fearful, dangerous situation and your thoughts are, "I can't believe this is happening. I'm going to get pummeled," those thoughts become a self-fulfilling prophecy. You need to decide to change those negative thoughts into positive conscious thoughts. "I am calm, in control. I can handle this situation. I have an escape plan." Those are positive conscious thoughts.

Have you ever walked away from an argument, you sit down, you calm down and you say to yourself, "I should have told him _____," "I should have said _____," "I should have_____, I should have _____." If you have, what that tells you, is that you did not have a plan for that low-level stressful event. If you had planned for it, you would have gone into autopilot mode based on your trained, planned response. Had you played a mental movie prior to that incident, your mental computer would have gone back to that data and automatically retrieved it in a fraction of a second. You would have responded based on how you trained your mind.

So let's take that example up a couple of notches. Somebody is in your face and calling you a no good son of a gun. How do you respond to that situation? Are you trained? Are you prepared? Have you thought through how you would respond? Do you go back into your mental computer, and get that information so that you can respond appropriately?

What if someone is trying to physically attack you—how do you respond to it? Do you submit? Do you give up? Do you freeze? Do you try to run? If you can't run, do you try to physically defend yourself? What is your response to this stressful situation? Think through that scenario. What would you do to escape? If you need some actual self-defense moves, go to my website, www.PersonalSafetyTraining.com. I've posted videos demonstrating self-defense and escape tactics that you can practice with someone you trust. You can also buy self-defense videos and personal defensive tools there.

I train people how to teach personal safety courses, self-defense, defensive tactics, and certain law enforcement and security topics. Part of every course is the importance of breathing, positive self-talk, and positive conscious thinking. There's nothing like having that prepared proactive response built-in to your amazing mind so that you respond automatically and appropriately to a stressful situation.

Manage Your Stress to Prepare Your Mind and Body

Now you know how to breathe properly, and you know how to write that mental movie. But there are ten more simple steps to take to manage your stress better. Because when your stress is managed better, you think straight. You're aware, you're vigilant, you'll avoid danger, be prepared to defend yourself if you have to, and be able to escape.

Stress Management Strategies

- Eating healthy
- Exercise regularly
- Stay hydrated
- Manage your time
- Hold positive thoughts
- Get touch therapy
- Have a support system
- Get in some recreation time!
- Spend time in nature
- Create a sacred space for yourself

You might be thinking, "Yeah, yeah. I know all that. I should be doing those things." If you take them as a whole, in other words, holistically, they add to the wholeness of your life and your ability to deal with those stressors that just happen, just the stress of life, not to mention the fear type of stress to dangerous situations. It will also increase your ability to be successful in the management of a stressful situation where you need to defend yourself or escape from an imminent assault situation.

Another thing to consider is being hyper-vigilant. Sometimes, when you're really tense, it can cause you to overreact to situations. Remember Erin "jumping out of her skin"? I asked her about that, because it seemed out of character for her:

> Oh yeah, I was just in the kitchen, but I *was* a total mess that day. I was super stressed about a dozen different things. No question that when that broom dropped, and it sounded like a gun shot, I was useless for a good ten seconds. I thought about that, too. I thought—what if a sound like that had been followed by one of my kids screaming in pain? Would I have been able to respond like I should?
>
> I *really* think about that when I'm out and about. I've gotten better about it, but I know if I'm deep in thought and not being aware, and not being vigilant, and somebody steps out from behind a car in a parking lot, and I jump... I mean, I'm just not safe. Being super tensed almost makes me act hyper-vigilant.

Remember that hyper-vigilance is counter-productive; it'll make you *less* able to respond appropriately. Just like being too stressed out will make you less able to respond appropriately. So manage your stress. It will keep you safe.

Let's look at those ten stress management techniques and see how they contribute to keeping yourself safe.

Eat Right to Stay Sharp

Proper nutrition and healthy eating habits can help you get through stressful times. Eating well will increase your physical, mental and emotional stamina. Fueling yourself with food high in nutrients can boost your immune system, help you maintain a healthy weight and help you feel better about yourself.

You heard this as a kid—if you want strong muscles and bones, you need to eat good food. A healthy diet will also prepare your body for stress; when your body is fueled with good, wholesome food, you're better able to deal with the everyday stressors.

Also, when you eat right, you're much sharper mentally. When you load up on empty calories, you literally can't think straight. Or if you skip eating altogether. When you're blood sugar is out of whack, your brain cannot function properly. In fact, people having severe diabetic episodes are sometimes mistaken for being drunk! How can you be aware and vigilant if you're foggy-brained?

There are literally hundreds of books on diet and nutrition. I am not advocating any particular diet or eating plan. Do some research, consult with your physician, and figure out what foods work best for you, what foods bog you down and make you feel lethargic, dull and slow. Eat foods that give you energy and make you feel vibrant.

I have done the Ironman Triathlon three times, and I still have room for improvement in my eating habits. I have to constantly remind myself to eat more fruits and vegetables, and I love pizza as much as the next guy. It's all about moderation, though, and making sure that I stay sharp enough to keep myself and my loved ones safe.

Exercise to Stay Safe

You don't have to be a triathlete or a black belt to be able to protect yourself. In fact, most of the self-defense techniques you can learn at our website (www.PersonalSafetyTraining.com) or (www.AVADEtraining.com) or from our videos don't require anything more than common sense and practice. Some of our training seminars are open to the public, too, so you can enroll in one if you really want to become proficient. And you certainly don't need to be a marathon runner to be able to get away from an attacker. But being fit skews the odds in your favor.

Frequent exercise is one of the best physical stress reduction techniques. Exercise not only improves your health and reduces stress, it also relaxes tensed muscles and helps you sleep better—and fatigue is one of those underrated handicaps. When you're tired, you're not as aware as you may need to be. And, just like eating right, regular exercise is good for your brain. It helps blood flow to your brain, and that will sharpen your awareness and your vigilance.

Physically fit people have less severe physiological responses when under stress than those who are not physically fit. For me, regular exercise has become habitual. I love to exercise. Not just for my body and how it feels, but for my mental capabilities. When I get done running, doing martial arts, biking or swimming, I just feel better on the inside. Any stress that I have, I seem to leave out there on the trails that I run. I leave it at the gym. I leave it in the pool. It helps me cope.

Exercise is important for your brain capacity, too. In his book, *Brain Rules: 12 Principles for Surviving and Thriving at Work, Home, and School*, Dr. John Medina states that cardiovascular exercise, two to three times a week, reduces your likelihood to develop Alzheimer's, dementia and stroke by over 50%. This guy is a molecular biologist, and he's found in his studies that regular exercise is what you're built for. That's how humanity evolved. Primitive humans had to exercise to adapt, to overcome, to survive, to evolve. Modern Americans just don't exercise enough. Primitive humans had to walk miles and miles a day just for food and survival. Today, we measure distance from here to the refrigerator. Countless doctors have told me that if they could prescribe one thing that would prevent most stress, it would be exercise.

Make it a habit. Make it a hobby. Make it fun to exercise to help reduce your stress. Keeping fit will help keep you safe.

Headache? Drink Some Water

Dehydration is one of the most common causes of headaches. I don't know about you, but when my head is pounding, I'm not particularly aware or vigilant. Dehydration can also reduce mental acuity and cause nausea, constipation and irritability. Water is essential to your well-being.

Conventional wisdom says you should drink half your body weight in ounces of water. For example, a 150-pound person should be drinking 75 ounces of water. I weigh approximately 180 pounds. That means I should be drinking 90 ounces of water. Now, that doesn't include coffee, soft drinks or alcohol. That's just pure, clean water.

I know I don't get enough water. That's a habit that I'm working on, increasing my water intake. I'll know that I haven't had enough water on particular days because I'll start to get a little bit of a headache, which is good feedback for me. That says, "David, you need to get some more water in you."

Again, your personal safety is mostly about your own awareness and vigilance. You need to be sharp to make safe decisions, so drink your water!

Late Again!

When I am teaching classes, and people rush in at the last minute, or late, I know that those people will not be focused for a while. When you're rushing around, you're not in the moment. You're not in the present. And what does that mean? You're not aware. You're not necessarily safe.

Managing your time will help reduce your stress, as well. You ever get to the end of your day and you say to yourself, "Ah! I should have given her a call!" "I should have sent him an e-mail!" "I should have picked that stuff up at the store!" You just "should have" all over yourself, as the saying goes, and that causes more stress in your life. But planning your day— making a prioritized to-do list, for instance—can help you accomplish more and feel more in control of your life. It minimizes conflicts and last minute rushes. Learn to say "no." You only have so much time, so use it effectively. You'll feel less stressed, more focused, and more aware.

I Think I Can... I Think I Can...

Negative thoughts create energy that can affect you in many ways that can cause you additional stress. Develop the habit of turning negative thoughts around: "I'll never get this done on time!" becomes "I can get this done on time, and the end product will be exactly what I need." Frame your thoughts in a positive way to reduce stress in your life. Maintain and increase positive thoughts by listening to uplifting music, reading inspirational books, spending time with positive people, and using positive affirmations.

Make it a habit, so when you're faced with a dire situation, you're in the habit of seeing the upside, the positive way out. Instead of, "This guy is going to kill me," which will probably make you freeze up, you will automatically go to, "I need to escape NOW—how can I do that?"

Can you measure the power of a thought? I certainly believe you can. In the secular book *Power vs. Force: The Hidden Determinants of Human Behavior*, by David Hawkins, he teaches a method of measuring the power of thoughts called kinesiological muscle testing.

This method uses your own body, and it's best done with two people. One person will stand with their feet shoulder width apart holding their right arm out straight, with their fist closed. The second person will push down on the wrist of the arm that is extended, using just two fingers. As individual #2 pushes down on individual #1's extended arm, individual #1 resists having their arm pushed down. That's the initial part of the test, which determines the ability of the person to resist.

Now, you add some thoughts to it. Have individual #1 focus on a negative thought, somebody who has hurt them in the past, somebody who has caused them harm, who's made them feel ashamed of themselves. (If a person is having a hard time thinking about negative, just have them think of Charles Manson or Hitler, someone truly horrible.) As individual #1 is thinking about this upsetting person or situation, individual #2 pushes down on their extended arm. Most people will "go weak," they will not have the ability to resist, and individual #2 will easily push their arm down with just their two fingers. That's the second part of the test.

The third part of the test is to have the individual #1 hold their arm out again, and make a fist while they think positive thoughts. The highest energy in the universe is love, so have the person to think about a loved one, their children, their parents, their spouse—anyone who makes them feel happy. Now individual #2 pushes down on their arm. Almost unanimously those thoughts of power and love bring strength, and individual #1's arm cannot be pushed down.

After reading *Power vs. Force* I found this technique of measuring thoughts to be quite remarkable. Literally think about what your thoughts are—are they positive or are they negative. Think of this in a dangerous situation: if you're defending yourself, you need to be thinking, "I can win this;" if you're trying to escape, you need to be thinking, "I can outrun him," "I can get away." Thinking positively literally makes you stronger.

Everybody Needs a Hug

Our sense of touch is also a management technique for reducing stress. Touch is the first sense to develop in humans. It is essential to your health and well-being; babies will fail to thrive and even die without an adequate amount of physical contact. Adults can become depressed and even ill if they are isolated from this most basic of human needs.

Kids inherently know how to ask for this. Don't your children climb up into your lap, looking for that touch? My daughters are grown and they (thankfully) still want hugs from their dad. Even shaking hands, that physical contact, is much needed in all of our lives.

Renowned family therapist Virginia Satir says that you need four hugs a day just for maintenance. You need eight hugs a day to move forward, and up to twelve hugs a day to thrive. How many hugs are you getting in a day? Are you even maintaining? Are you moving forward or are you thriving? Are you getting enough touch therapy?

People are starting to realize how much stress they release when their bodies are touched and massaged; that tension gets worked out of your body, and you feel so much better. In fact, massage has become a thriving industry in our country. But just the simple act of touching and hugging will help you in your ability to manage the stress of life. Sometimes, don't you just need that hug? I know I do. And again, when you're more relaxed, you're more aware. Remember, being tensed up can make you hyper-sensitive, distracted—and vulnerable.

Lean on... Someone

Having a strong support system will help you in times of stress. When my father died, when I got divorced, I sought out people who would support me, people I could talk to, whom I could trust as part of my support system. Study after study shows that people who have supportive family, friends and even co-workers are happier and more productive.

It's nice to have people around you who lift you up, give you ideas, support you, help you stay stable when you feel like your world is caving in around you. It doesn't really matter where you get that support—from family, friends, co-workers, whomever—you just need to get it. You really need to have these people around you.

Also, be part of somebody's support system. Give support to others who are having trying times. Be there to lend an ear, open your heart, to encourage, to support, to care. That's what a support system is all about. Having a good support system is a way to create and produce more positive energy, increased strength, less stress, more focus, more awareness and an increase of vigilance.

Enjoy Yourself!

I love to relax and enjoy recreation. Look at the word: it's literally "re-create." Recreate yourself as a relaxed person. It's how you can recharge your batteries. It's about having fun. We become so serious as we get older, and we forget about that playfulness inside of all of us.

Do anything you like: sports, arts, crafts, games, dancing—any activity that involves participation. Play. Have fun. Reduce your stress by just enjoying yourself. Be present, too. Don't think about work, or bills, or that bathroom you need to paint. Recreating is a great time to practice just being present.

Get Back to Nature

When you enjoy nature to reduce your stress, you realize the abundance that's around you. For a lot of us, it's the lack of abundance that's causing you stress—lack of money, lack of time, lack of love. But when you go into nature, when you look into the trees, the mountains, the flowers, you look into the ocean or the lakes or the rivers, and you realize how abundant life really is.

I spend all day in classrooms, conference rooms, board rooms, under fluorescent lights, breathing recycled air. Often on lunch, or before I head back to my hotel room, I'll go find a patch of grass, take my shoes off , and just get my feet into the grass so my body can be in touch with nature.

When I'm home, I head to a park that's right on the lake. It's a beautiful place. It's a hill with paths all over it, and this park is sacred to me. There's a loop that's 2.2 miles, and it takes me anywhere from twenty to thirty minutes to hike or run it. When I'm going around that hill, I just release. I just release the stress and it's not part of me during those moments. When I'm done with that loop, I leave something up there. I leave my stress. That fresh, clean air, that feeling that God is at work there, it clears my mind. When my mind's clear, I can get clarity in solving my problems and dealing with the issues that I have in my life.

God's abundance of vitality and wonder is everywhere. Just go out and look at it. Open your window. Look at the trees, look at the flowers, look at your grass, and, if you can, get out into the woods. Go to the mountains. When you get into nature, you just feel better, and when you feel better, you have less stress.

Sacred Spaces

A sacred space is any place where you're temporarily sealed off from the world. I just described one of my sacred places, that lake-side hill where I run and hike. But a sacred place can be a room, a special chair, an activity or just a state of mind. The idea is that when you're in a sacred space, whatever you're doing becomes a meditation or a peaceful state for your mind and your body.

Creating and maintaining your sacred space is a great way to reduce stress. I'm not talking about religion or philosophy here. What I'm talking about is a physical, sacred space for you. Whatever that is, whatever that place is, or that activity is, when you do that, it allows you to release stress, to become one, a wholeness of your mind, body and your spirit. It allows that to happen. So find that sacred space. When you know how it feels to be completely at ease, totally relaxed, it's a lot easier to bring that out into the world with you. Aside from being relaxed, you will feel more confident in yourself. And you now know that a confident presence is a huge deterrent to predators.

I'll bet you never considered how being relaxed, happy and confident can keep you safe, did you? But it all ties together. Being relaxed, being present, and your new-found awareness and vigilance become part of your everyday reality, and keep you safer.

When You Need Help, Get It

I believe it's important to make note here that a person who is involved in a highly stressful situation should seek some type of treatment. Getting that out of you is vitally important. I know most people have coping abilities to deal with stress, but if you're involved in a situation where you were hurt, assaulted, whether that was physically, sexually, emotionally—whatever the type of assault that hurt you, you need to seek some type of help. Individuals who are exposed to an assault or even a witness to an assault should consider some level of critical incident debriefing or counseling. A woman who was attacked and beaten told me this story:

> I thought PTSD [Post Traumatic Stress Disorder] was something for Vietnam vets. I had no idea it could come from one incident. For years afterward—probably ten years—anytime a man raised his voice to me, even just an unhappy or frustrated customer at work, or a man drove aggressively around me, my heart would pound, my face would flush, and I would be sure, *sure,* that the pissed-off guy was going to come back and beat the snot out of me. I was more combative with men right off the bat—which seems counter-intuitive—but ANY kind of confrontation equaled, in my mind, a potential pummeling.
>
> I got married six years after I had been beaten, and it probably took another five or six years for my husband to be able to come up behind me and put his arms around me, even around my waist. You know how sometimes a guy will stand behind a woman, and wrap his arms around her neck loosely, to cuddle? I could NOT handle that. Even when I *knew* it was my husband—who is the sweetest, gentlest man in the world—my heart would pound, I would break out into a sweat immediately, and I would start to shake.
>
> I wish I'd known at the time that I had PTSD. It would have saved me years of stress. When Dave taught me about hyper-vigilance, I realized I lived in that state for years. So, ironically, I was *less* safe from being so paranoid.

If you've been involved in a serious situation—even a bad car accident—get some help right away. Find a counselor who specializes in Post-Traumatic Stress Disorder (PTSD), or who is skilled in Critical Incident Stress Debriefing (CISD).

CISD is a specific technique designed to assist others in dealing with physical or psychological symptoms that are generally associated with critical incident trauma exposure. Debriefing allows those involved with the incident to process the event and reflect on its impact. Research on the effectiveness of critical incident debriefing techniques has demonstrated that individuals who are provided critical incident stress debriefing within a 24 to 72 hour window after the critical incident and experience will experience less short-term and long-term crisis reactions and psychological trauma. So if you're involved in some type of situation where you are hurt physically, mentally or sexually, seek counseling. Get some type of debriefing.

The final extent of a traumatic situation may never be known or realistically estimated in terms of trauma, loss and grief. In the aftermath of any critical incident, psychological reactions are quite common and are fairly predictable. Critical incident stress debriefing can be a valuable tool following a traumatic event.

Many agencies and employers now have an employee assistance program (EAP) for counseling and debriefing. At the medical center where I worked in security, anytime *anyone* was involved in a security incident as part of a responding team, we would meet after the incident and do a short debriefing, just talking about the incident and how it went. That time spent talking about the incident and the experience was very helpful. That way we could go on with our daily duties and not carry anything around with us.

Whether you're a witness or a victim, I would encourage you to seek some level of counseling or debriefing following a traumatic incident.

"The best way to block a blow? Don't be there."

-A 26-year veteran of a Bay Area police force
SWAT and Defensive Tactics Instructor

Chapter 7

Time and Distance

I travel to Los Angeles a few times a month. When I get picked up at LAX, I'll ask my driver how far it is to my hotel, the hospital, or corporation where I'll be presenting. In LA, the answer to that question is usually, "Do you want to know the actual distance in miles? Or how long it will take to get there?" In LA, it all depends on the time of day and how bad the traffic is. It can take an hour to get three miles if there's an accident or rush hour traffic. Time and distance are relative.

Early on in my martial arts training, I learned a lot about distance and timing. The downfall to all martial arts, or martial science systems, is this: if I am close enough to strike my opponent, he is close enough to strike me. That's the paradox of martial science right there. That's why, in our infinite wisdom, Humanity has created weapons to extend our distance from an opponent or an assailant; weapons are just an extension of your hands.

People always ask me, "How much distance do I need from someone who is physically combative?" The answer is, as much distance as possible. The more distance you have, the better the possibility that you'll prevent an attack and be able to get away from an aggressor.

I train people in a program called AVADE® Workplace Violence prevention. AVADE® includes a "distance guideline" for nurses and other health care staff. When dealing with people who are in the stress stage, you should maintain a distance of approximately four feet. From that distance, you have time to move, to disengage, to create some space. When dealing with people who are angry, you would increase that buffer to about six feet. If things escalate, and the person becomes physically aggressive, now the health care worker has more time because he/she has more distance to stay away from an attack and escape.

Distance is the key. It gives you time to respond, react, get away. Imagine that you have the ability to use time and distance to your advantage. Just start with that—imagine it.

Time Is on Your Side in the OODA Loop

U.S. Air Force Colonel John Boyd was a fighter pilot who studied air combat. He found that in the midst of air-to-air combat, while going in excess of the speed of sound, the person who makes the quickest decisions ultimately wins the air battle.

He figured out that we go through four processes in order to ultimately make decisions and to act upon those decisions: Observe, Orient, Decide and Act. That's the OODA Loop. What Colonel Boyd found is that *time* is the dominant parameter. The individual who goes through the OODA cycle in the shortest time prevails, because his opponent is caught responding to situations that have already changed.

That first "O" is for observation. This is the collection of relevant data by means of your senses. That primary sense is going to be your sense of sight to capture what is going on at that moment.

The second "O" is orientation, which means analyzing what you've just observed, processing the data to form your mental perspective of what is happening.

The "D" in the OODA cycle represents your decision about your course of action based on your current mental perspective. This is the cognitive response that you're going through to make a decision. Should I do something? And if so, what should I do?

The last part of the OODA cycle is the action you take. Making a decision is the prelude to an action, but you have to physically do whatever you decided to do.

The OODA Loop works for Air Force pilots, but it also works for you in your personal safety. The key is speed, remember. So the more you plan and prepare, the more you play mental movies—what would I do if some one grabbed me? What would I do if someone rushed me?—the more you will train your mind to respond, so you move through the OODA Loop quicker than your assailant.

Distance Gives You Time

I'd like you to do a little exercise to prove to yourself that time and distance can give you safety. You need a partner for this. Obviously, if you don't have a partner it's going to be a little bit difficult to do this exercise.

Get a partner, and stand and face them directly at a distance where you can touch your partner's shoulder, so you're fairly close. (If you have any jewelry or anything that can cut or scrape or scratch your partner, remove it.) Now reach out with one of your hands and touch your partner's shoulder. Your partner's job is to move away from that simulated attack or block it. Caution here, you are just trying to touch the other person's shoulder—not hit or strike them. Again, your partner blocks the attack or moves away from the attack. Now reverse the roles; let your partner attack you and see if you can block it or move away from it.

I've done this with thousands of people, and they all discovered what you just realized: arm's length is too close. Within arm's reach, you're in the strike zone, and action beats reaction within the strike zone.

Now, you and your partner take a small step back, so you're approximately a foot past your arm's length, about 3 1/2 to 4 feet apart. Now you can't reach your partner's shoulder. To touch their shoulder now, you need to step forward—but they have a lot more time to block or to move out of the way of the attack.

Try that a few times, then switch roles and have your partner attack you, so you can practice either blocking or moving away from the attack.

You can increase the distance out to 6 feet, 8 feet, 10 feet, etc. But you get the point. The more distance you have between you and an attacker, the more time you have to get away, to escape, to do something.

In the law enforcement world, they've done different studies that show that officers need lots of distance to defend themselves. These studies have shown that a person can cover 21 feet in approximately 1.5 seconds. So officers are trained that, in an attack situation with a club, a stick or a knife, they are justified in using deadly force if their attacker is less than 21 feet away.

Dennis Tueller, a retired Salt Lake City police lieutenant, was integral in educating law enforcement and the judicial system of this 21 feet rule. When training officers in this principle, they use what is now referred to as the "Tueller Drill."

In this training drill, first an attacker would start to close in, getting ready to attack the police officer with a club, stick or knife. The officers are prompted to draw their handgun, shoot twice to center body, and then move away from the attack. The drill starts at a distance of 3 feet, goes out to 5 feet, 10 feet, then 15 feet, and then 21 feet. Officers find that at the distance of 3 feet and 5 feet, they just don't have time to draw their gun and respond with the appropriate force against that attack. Even if they could draw their gun and maybe even shoot, if they didn't step out of the attack zone, they still failed because the carry through of the attack would still hit the police officer. At the distances of 10 and 15 feet, more officers were successful, but a pretty small percentage. At a distance of 21 feet, most officers had enough time to respond to the deadly force attack.

Facing an Armed Attacker

So how do you defend yourself against a club or a stick? I hope you've gotten this by now, but I'll say it again:

Your best defense is to escape, escape, escape. Run away. Create distance. The more distance, the better.

Obviously, that's not always possible, and sometimes you may need to defend yourself.

Most people's worst nightmare is to face someone armed with a gun. After the massacres at Columbine High School, Virginia Tech and Ft. Hood, it's foremost in people's minds. It's called an "active shooter" situation, and I'll cover that more extensively in the next chapter.

So, if somebody puts a gun in your face and wants your money, what should you do? Give them your money! Give them your purse. Give them your belongings. That stuff can all be replaced. Remember what my friend, that retired Bay Area police officer, said about muggings: he's seen too many women beaten to a pulp because they wouldn't give up a purse. So make that decision right now. Play that mental movie. You're facing someone with a gun and they want your money and valuables, give them up. It's not worth the risk.

What if it's not a simple robbery? What if you're facing someone who really intends to hurt you, and they have a gun aimed at you? I'm talking about a gun threat, not a gun attack, which is an "active shooter." If someone is threatening you with a gun, and wants more than your belongings, know this: it is very difficult for a shooter to hit a moving target. I'm a hunter, and I and other hunters will tell you, once that deer or elk starts to move, you've probably lost your prey. Even police officers who practice shooting regularly will tell you, once you start to move the target around, it becomes very difficult to get a shot in, let alone a deadly shot.

Don't make it easy for the gunman. Get to safe cover immediately, if you can. What's safe cover? It's not a cardboard box. I'm talking about getting behind a thick door, behind a thick wall, behind a car, a large object that bullets cannot penetrate. A safe room, a panic room, somewhere where you're fully protected, fully covered from the attack.

If you cannot get to safe cover immediately, do not, do NOT, hide behind a cardboard box, or its equivalent. The girls in the library of Columbine High School had been taught only one disaster scenario—the duck and cover. So they ducked and covered under the tables in the library. Eric Harris and Dylan Klebold, the killers in Columbine, walked up and shot them pointblank. Again, in the next chapter, we'll go more into depth about what to do in an active shooter situation. Now, I'm talking about someone trying to rob you who is escalating, maybe a mentally ill person, that kind of thing, not someone who has planned an attack, like the Columbine shooters, or the Virginia Tech shooter.

Without the ability to seek cover in a gun situation, your best defense is to move. Run, zigzag, jump, keep moving until you're away and in a covered position. A gunman walks into the room I'm in right now, I'm going to jump, move, roll, do everything I possibly can to make it difficult for the gunman to hit me, to shoot me. Escape!

Anything Can Be a Weapon

Despite the extensive media coverage of shootings, they are actually not all that common. The weapons that I'm most concerned with in our society are edged weapons; that is, knives, because they're so prevalent. Think about the edged weapons that you have in your home right now— kitchen knives, scissors, screwdrivers. Most people have dozens. What about pens or pencils— they have a sharp end that can penetrate the human body. I'm far more concerned about those because they're everywhere. Just about anything can be sharpened and used as a weapon against another person, toothbrushes, shards of metal, plastic. I'm not intending to scare you here, I just want to increase your awareness of how many edged weapons are around you at this moment.

The minimum distance that you want from a person with an edged weapon is 21 feet. Why? Because we just found out that the average person can cover 21 feet in approximately 1.5 seconds, which is seven paces. They can get to you quickly.

If you can't get away, you're going to need to defend yourself. I've been teaching edged-weapon defenses for many years, and the one thing I make sure people understand is this: you are going to get cut. Plain and simple, in dealing with an edged weapon, if you don't have enough distance, and you can't get away, you're going to get cut. Period.

I know that's scary. But it's important to understand that getting cut is NOT the same thing as getting *killed*. You can minimize how bad or how deeply you're injured in a simple way: drop to the ground. Drop to the ground on your side, your non-dominant side down (so if you're right-handed, drop onto your left side, if possible), and kick the knee of the aggressor with your dominant foot (sidekick). Now remember, that's last resort. Run away if you can! Escape is always your best defense. But if you can't get away, drop to the ground and kick the assailant's knee as hard as you can. This protects your upper body, the vital areas of the body. If your hands, arms or feet get cut, they have very little chance of hitting an artery. You can even grab the knife, grab it by the blade, if you have to.

Deadly Thrown Objects

How would you like to get hit with a 93 mile-an-hour fastball? Baseball players have been hit in the face and it's ended their career. In some cases, it can shatter the face. But you're probably not going to encounter a major league pitcher hurling a fastball at your face. What you should be concerned about is people throwing common, everyday objects at you.

During my years in hospital security services, we were often concerned with chairs getting thrown at us. The good thing about that is a person usually can't throw a chair very far. What they can throw a fair distance are tray tables, computers, one of my officers got a VCR right in the face. He got hurt pretty bad, because he was fairly close, trying to apprehend an aggressive individual.

Again, you want to maintain enough distance to get away from that type of attack. Do you need 21 feet? Well, in some cases, you might, depending on what's being thrown at you. But sometimes being close to a person might even be better.

The medical center where I worked has many behavioral health units, which are a type of on-site psychiatric unit. Our security office got a call one day to restrain a young girl, 13 or 14 years old. As I moved closer to her, she picked up a chair. Even a 14-year-old girl can do some damage with a chair. As she raised it above her head to throw it at me, I used my hand and blocked her at the elbow, which kept her arm from going forward. Well, that prevented that attack upon me and my partner was able to get the chair that was now behind her head and bring it back down.

Getting close and blocking is a last resort. Again, DISTANCE is your friend. Create space. Thrown objects can be dangerous.

Hey, Look Over There!

Remember that OODA Loop? The person who responds quicker wins. So how do you interrupt someone else's OODA Loop, force them to start over before they can decide and act? You distract them.

A loud scream or yell can cause a momentary delay of the attacker. He was set on a course of action, now he has to respond to a new piece of information. Distractions buy you time. Time allows you to create distance. Fractions of a second that distractions can buy may allow you to escape, or allow you to defend.

When I worked at the medical center, we got a call to go to the Emergency Room where a patient who'd been put on a psychiatric hold had become physically aggressive.

When my four security officers and I arrived, the man was standing on the bed, in a fighting stance. We'd been instructed by the clinical staff that we needed to restrain him now. Obviously, none of us really wanted to get hit as we tried to step in and grab one of his limbs to get control of him.

So I distracted him. I said, "Hey, look. If you don't get down and lay on your back, Jim is going to get you." As I said that, I looked at, and pointed towards, Jim, one of my security partners. What did the aggressor's eyes do as I said, "Jim is going to get you," and looked and pointed at Jim? He looked at Jim. I knew that was coming. I knew that he would respond that way. So in that exact moment that he diverted his attention, I grabbed him. In that split second when his attention was diverted, his awareness was re-directed, we got a hold of him and restrained him.

Any little distraction can work to your advantage. If a gun-wielding mugger demands your wallet or purse, toss it slightly away. It will distract him, giving you more time to create distance. Some so-called security experts out there say that you shouldn't toss your wallet or your purse. You should hand it over to the bad guy. I totally disagree with that. Distractions work and they work well. Distractions affect the senses, it takes time for the mind to process the new information. In all the self-defense techniques that I teach in law enforcement, security, military, the private sector and even with civilians, I cover distractions with everything—all techniques. There is no exception. Distractions give you time to create distance.

Sound

Have you ever been startled by somebody screaming or yelling? Or the loud noise of somebody dropping something behind you? The sound of tires squealing, emergency sirens—all those noises distract you, don't they? They cause you to hesitate for just a second. It sends you back to the beginning of that OODA Loop.

We always use sound distractions in control techniques and defense techniques. You've probably heard Karate people yell "Hi-ya!" That's not just grand-standing; there's a purpose to that loud burst of sound and air that comes out of the martial artist. It's a distraction that causes a momentary delay in their opponent before they attack.

So use sound distractions. Even if it's psychological distraction, not just a scream or a yell. Ask somebody who's threatening you an off-the-wall question. "When was the last time you bought socks?" "Do you know how to make chocolate chip cookies?" The person involuntarily processes that information—they're distracted. That gives you time.

When I distracted that psychiatric patient who was standing on the bed, I spoke, distracting him with noise; I gave him information he had to process, and I diverted his eyes. And it worked.

Whistles and boat horns are popular in rape defense training. They're effective, and definitely distracting—also, those sounds alert others of a confrontation.

If you're going to yell and scream, should you yell "help"? Actually, no. "Help" is not conducive to your vocal chords when you're stressed. Words like "Stop!" "No!" and "Fire!" are conducive to stressed vocal chords. Make the words "no" and "stop" habitual. Teach your mothers, your daughters, your sisters, all the females in your life. I have friends who have two little girls. One is a very quiet child. A couple of times a year, her mom will make her practice yelling "NO!" as loud as she can (while explaining that this is what you do if someone does something that scares you, tries to touch you, or tries to grab you). The mom says it makes her daughter visibly uncomfortable, but she encourages her to continue to do it, to make it habitual for her daughter's safety.

I was in Seattle recently, working with billing and reception people at a hospital. This class was all women, and we were practicing yelling "No!" and "Stop!" I was prompting them, "On the count of three we're all going to yell 'Stop!'" I counted off one, two, three and the women said, "stop," barely loud enough for me to hear. So I said, "Come on, ladies. We've got to do better at this. We've got to get some loud vocal noise in here. We have to express some energy." It took several more attempts, but they finally got loud, got strong, created a distraction. In fact, another trainer doing a completely different topic in another classroom across the hallway, ran across into the room and said, "Is everything okay in here?" It was a perfect illustration that yelling "No!" or "Stop!" will bring someone to your aid.

Practice yelling "No!" and "Stop!" so that you have that assertive presence when you need to distract an assailant.

Physical Distractions

Another distraction that you can use is any type of body movement. If I stick my hand up, my palm out in front a person's face, that's a distraction. If I stomp my foot, point in a certain direction, lean to the side as though I'm looking behind an assailant, that will distract them. Looking around them might even get them to turn their back for a split second— which would give me time to escape and create distance.

I have used these types of distractions for years in my martial arts competitions. I would stomp my foot, move my hands a certain way. Boxers do it, too; it's called bobbing and weaving.

I remind ladies all the time that they often have a distraction right in their hands:

> You're walking through the parking lot, you've got your cup of Starbucks in your hand, and all of sudden here comes "Mr. Weirdo." Well, you've got two distraction choices: you can throw the whole coffee cup towards the aggressor, but you can also throw the contents into the aggressor's face. That momentary delay can give you valuable time to get away.

Temporarily Blinding the Assailant

One of my favorite personal defensive tools is a flashlight. Police officers often carry large, heavy, extremely bright flashlights. If you've ever had one shined in your face, you'll know how distracting it is. Any flashlight is an excellent safety device, even if it's not a potential weapon like the ones police carry. Think of this: you're walking out to your car, it's evening, it's low light hours, you've got a flashlight to lead the way. If someone approaches you who gives you an uneasy feeling, you can shine that flashlight into their eyes, which causes that momentary distraction. They see spots, which gives you time to get away.

Get yourself one of these new flashlights that's got a very bright light, a real high beam with halogen bulbs. Some of them have lithium batteries. They only run about $10 or $20, and a lot of them are small enough to fit in your pocket. They're bright, so shining them in someone's eyes is like glancing up to the sun for a moment; it causes momentary blindness. In fact, an old warrior tactic is to always have the sun at your back. If you find yourself in a situation outside during the day, if possible, position yourself so the sun is in the aggressor's eyes.

I also teach the use of pepper spray. Pepper is an ancient form of distraction. Warriors have used it for thousands of years. The Chinese would grind pepper and burn it in big black boiling pots. When the wind conditions were right, that pepper smoke would blow into the enemy lines, causing a distraction and even temporarily blinding them. The Bushido and the Samurai ground pepper, and put it in blow tubes or rice paper packets and blew it into their opponent's eyes. Any kind of pepper in your eyes, whether it's cayenne, black pepper or pepper spray is going to cause some distraction[7]. And if an aggressor can't see, again, it gives you time to create distance.

Are you tired of hearing that yet? That your first job is to escape? And if you can't, distract your assailant, which can give you time to create distance and escape? I'm not tired of saying it. I hope you're not tired of hearing it. It could save your life one day.

---

[7] For civilian pepper spray products check out: www.sabrered.com or ww.guardpd.com

"When you fail to plan, you plan to fail."

— Anonymous

Chapter 8

Plan Your Escape

No one plans to be a victim of crime or violence. Who wants to plan for dealing with aggressive behavior, a violent situation, somebody trying to hurt me? You don't want to think about those things.

The only problem with that is, when something does happen, you're not prepared. You freeze. You panic. You become a victim. And you suffer far worse than if you would have thought it through, had a contingency plan, had some type of escape plan in place.

I think I've made it abundantly clear, by now, that your best plan of action to stay safe is to escape, escape, escape. Being aware and being vigilant help you avoid dangerous situations. You've learned that defense is your last resort. But when all that is said and done, you need a way out of the dangerous situation. You need an escape plan.

Have a Plan

Do you have an escape plan for a home invasion? When somebody tries to get into your home, you can certainly bet that their intentions are bad. What would you do if somebody tried to invade your vehicle, try to carjack you, or got in and held you at gunpoint or knifepoint and wanted you to drive to another location? What would you do? What's your escape plan?

What about work? If someone comes in shooting, do you know the best way out? Have a plan. For every aspect of your life. Make it habitual.

Develop an Escape Plan for Your Home

In 2005, convicted serial pedophile and child murderer Joseph Edward Duncan, III, came to my hometown of Coeur d'Alene, Idaho. He invaded a home, bludgeoned to death two adults and a teenaged boy in that home, and abducted two young children. It shook our community, and stole our sense of small-town safety.

It also really made me think: What would I do if somebody invaded my home? Until that point, I've never really thought about it. I was already a personal safety expert, traveling and teaching thousands of people a year how to deal with crime and aggression and violence—and I didn't have an escape plan for my own family in my own home.

I sat down with my family and we talked about it. My daughters were 12 and 16 at the time, and it frightened them at first. So I just presented it very matter-of-factly: "This is what we're going to do if somebody breaks into our house, invades our home, someone is going to yell out 'Intruder!' as loud as they can, to alert all the family members in our home. We're all going to meet in my bedroom, go out through the window, hang from the windowsill, and drop the three or four feet to the ground. We might bang up an ankle, hurt ourselves a little bit, but we'll be out of the house."

Our keyword is "intruder," and we never joke about that word. We never say it in jest. So pick a keyword, have a meeting place, and have a plan to get OUT of the house.

I know some people will say, "Well, screw that. I'm grabbing the gun. I'll get that son of a gun. I'll take care of this." Stop and think about that for a minute. What's more important—dealing with this bad guy in your home who has bad intentions, and who might have weapons as well, or getting your family out safely? Remember, *avoidance* will keep you safe. Don't confront an intruder if you can avoid it. Get your family out and get to safety.

Once outside the home you're going to go to neighbors, call the police and *stay safe*.

That's my escape plan for my home, for a home invasion. If my children were younger, I would have one of those rope ladders that are sold for fire drills in their room. If you have a baby, practice getting out a window and down the ladder with a doll in your arms. If there's an elderly person in your family who will need help getting out, practice by having your spouse pretend to need help, instead of the elderly person. (Don't make Grandma climb down a rope ladder until you have to.)

Can you escape in the dark? If you're escaping from your home, keeping it dark will work to your advantage; you know the lay of the land, the intruder probably doesn't. Do you know how many steps it takes, in complete darkness, to get to your bedroom? Do you know how many steps it takes to get out of your bedroom and to the back door, to the front door, or to the living room? Do you know how many stairs there are in your staircase?

I know; in my bedroom, it takes 11 steps to get from my side of the bed to my bedroom door. From there, across the landing is another 4 steps, down the stairs is 7, and at the bottom of the staircase I can go left to the front door, and that is approximately 9 or 10 steps. If I want to go out the backdoor, it means I have to go through the kitchen, which means I'm going to go about 7 steps, and then go left another 8 steps to the back door.

I've only done this a couple of times, and I counted the steps first in the light, obviously. Then I practiced a couple of times with the lights out just to see if I could do it. I got my kids involved, too, and they thought it was funny, but it made for an interesting 15 or 20 minutes one evening. It's another piece of my awareness of my environments and my escape routes, where our exits are. It's just a matter of practicing those things.

What are your escape routes? Right now, in the room you're sitting in, how could you get out of it? Did you lock the door you came in through? Is there another door you'd go out? Could you go out the window? Know your escape options.

Have an Escape Plan for Work

Sadly, workplace violence is a very real threat. When you're at work, do you have a plan to get out of your immediate area should a threatening, emergent or violent situation happen? Do you know how to get away?

Does your occupation have certain risks associated with it? Do you exchange cash? Are there narcotics or any types of drugs involved in your occupation that somebody might want? These are things you need to think about when it comes to workplace safety and our escape route, what you're going to do, how you're going to get out of there should an emergent or threatening situation happen. Just like with your purse, briefcase or bag, if someone is robbing you, let them have what they're after. It's not worth getting hurt. It's not worth getting injured or even dying.

Emergency department personnel have a high level of risk associated with their job, dealing with people who are emotional, who are stressed, who are under the influence of drugs or alcohol, who have mental health issues. There are definite risks associated with dealing with these folks. If you work in an ER, you need to think about how am I going to get away from this situation? How am I going to escape to a safe location? Remember time and distance—don't allow yourself to be backed into a corner with no exits if you're dealing with an agitated patient.

Maybe you don't work in an emergency room, or in a business that handles cash. Even in an office, there can be potentially dangerous situations.

Nancy, a friend of mine, told me this story:

> I had a co-worker named Julie. We were friendly, but I didn't know that Julie was dealing with domestic violence issues. One afternoon, Julie's live-in boyfriend showed up at our office. He was very demanding, and I was scared. I had no idea what was going on, why Julie's boyfriend was raging here in the middle of the office. It was really frightening.

You might think that your place of business is relatively safe, but you just don't realize, or always understand other people's problems and how those problems may affect you. When Nancy shared that story with me, I took the opportunity to ask her, how did you get away? She told me she didn't. I explained that her first priority was to get out of the strike zone, then out of the danger zone—the area—and call the police or security.

Have a plan in your workplace, know how you're going to get away, how you're going to escape. Have a Plan A. If that escape route is blocked, what's your Plan B? Your Plan C? Have a plan.

I teach supervisors, managers, and directors how to effectively conduct an employee disciplinary meeting, and terminations. Meet in a room with two exits. A lot of the older buildings were built many years ago, when they didn't have security in mind. Find a room that's safe if you think you'll be dealing with a dangerous individual. You'll want multiple exits to escape. Prepare ahead of time.

Escape Plans for Your Children's Schools

The Columbine massacre, the tragedy where Eric Harris and Dylan Klebold opened fire on innocent students, then killed themselves, has really brought an awareness to parents across our country that our schools are not necessarily always a safe place. You don't know all the kids going to the schools who are interacting with your kids.

In my daughter's high school, they have a "lockdown drill" that's very commonly used today. In this drill, there's an announcement, and the teacher is prompted to go and lock the door, and pull down the shades on the door. The kids then move to one side of the room, away from the doorway, and they remain quiet and just listen.

When she was in middle school, they did something very similar, and in the grade schools they do what will be similar to an earthquake drill in the schools in California where the kids would actually get under the desk. Whatever the drill is, I tell my daughter to do it. Go with what the school wants you to do.

But, I've taught her—and my college-age daughter—that if there's an active shooter, a person bent on hurting other people, she needs to have an escape plan. We talked about her classrooms, and I've seen them, so I know in most of her classes, she can climb out a window if needed.

We've talked about the pros and cons of escaping out into an area where there might be a potential attacker. Sometimes it's safer to stay put. Should it be a real deal and violence has erupted, you're hearing gunshots and screams and yells, would it be safe to run out of the classroom to a safe area, a parking lot or another room? Well, probably not, because you might be running in the direction of the aggressive individual, towards the violence. So staying put is often good. That's what you want to do. You want to barricade yourself in and stay put until the police tell you it's safe.

Seung-hui Cho, the killer at Virginia Tech, used a ruse to gain entry to more classrooms: he pounded on the door and said he needed help. In one case, he did get in and opened fire on the students. Other classrooms denied him entry, thankfully. They locked and barricaded the door, preventing him from entering. That was exactly the right thing to do, because those classes had no fatalities.

Escape Plans for Public Places

Public places are another thing to think about. You go to the mall, you go out into the public, you go to a park—where's your escape route? What's your exit? What's your strategy?

Consider this: you're at the mall, shopping with your family. You have your two small children with you and an older aunt. You hear what you believe to be gunshots from the west end of the mall. You're in a hallway a few hundred feet from the food court, with three retail stores in between. Your nearest exit is in the direction where the gunshots are coming from. What do you do? What's your escape route?

That sounds all-too familiar, doesn't it? When I give this scenario to people, it really gets them thinking, "What would I do? I've got my kids with me. I've got an elderly aunt who can't move very well. My escape route is where the gunshots are coming from. There are some stores in between the area. Could I go into the store and find a place to hide, to seek cover?" That's a good answer, isn't it? And, of course, once inside the store, you're going to alert authorities, you're going to protect yourself, you're going to let other people know what's happening. Protect yourself, protect your kids and your elderly aunt.

What are some other public places that you go into? The grocery store, the gas station, restaurants, hospitals or medical centers. What is your escape route in these places if you need to get away quickly?

For me, it's become habitual to find an escape route in any new environment. I stay in hotels almost every week, and it's a conditioned habit that I just look for exit signs. I know how I'm going to get away, where the stairwells are, what my plan of action is should something happen. Can I get out the windows? Is there another doorway I can go down? Is it safe to get into the elevator?

In any new physical environment—a new office, a new house, a new vehicle, a place you've never shopped before—think about your escape route. Put the data in and then forget about it. Remember, it's all about awareness, not hyper-vigilance. That information will be there in the storage banks of your amazing mind when you need it.

Escape Plans for Relationships

Have you ever gotten an invitation to go out—to a party, or a club, or a sporting event—and you had an uneasy feeling? But it was a touchy situation, and you didn't know how to get out of it? Guess what? You're allowed to say, "No, thanks." You don't need to explain that that particular club is always in the news for bar fights. Or that the guy throwing the party has a friend who's a mean drunk. Or that the fans for that sport team are just way too rowdy for your comfort zone. Just say no.

Some friends of mine had to go out-of-state for a family wedding recently. One groomsman was my friend's brother-in-law, and he's an unpredictable drunk. My friend told me about his and his wife's escape plan if things got ugly.

My wife's brother was getting married, and her other brother was a groomsman. This other brother, "Uncle Joey," is volatile. Many years ago, before I met her, he actually beat her unconscious when he was in a drunken rage. Needless to say, we are VERY careful around him, and just avoid him whenever possible. In 15 years, I have never seen him sober.

The reception was in the same hotel we were all staying in, so my wife and I made plans to get out of there if he got out of control. We knew where both exits were, we knew where the other elevators were, so we could get far away from the reception if we needed to. We talked to our 8-year-old daughter and explained that if Uncle Joey made her at all uncomfortable, to get away from him immediately and find one of us. (We were never far, though, obviously. In all that chaos, it would have been easy to lose a kid.) Free booze was flowing, but neither of us drank more than champagne. We wanted to have fun, and we did, but we also knew we needed to stay aware.

As it turned out, Uncle Joey was a happy drunk that night—and I mean *drunk*. He started drinking at noon, and the wedding was at four, the reception at six. But there were no incidents. And because we planned, because we talked about all contingencies, my wife and I were able to relax and enjoy the wedding and reception.

You might need an escape plan *from* a relationship—even if it's a relationship you didn't want in the first place. My friend Denise came to me because of an individual, an acquaintance who just didn't want to let go.

I met him at my hair salon. My hairdresser is a really good friend; our families hang out together, so I drop by his salon a lot. This guy was a handyman kind of guy, and he was around the salon doing some work on the equipment. He made me uncomfortable almost immediately. He lived near my friend's salon, so when I'd drop by, he'd see my car there, and he would just show up. Somehow he got my cell phone number. He'd call at strange times and ask me where I was, who I was with, and it just was very strange. I mean, I'm happily married. He seemed to have some substance abuse issues, too, and he was just weird.

Denise consulted me and said, "Dave, I know you're a personal safety expert, and this guy is practically stalking me. I told him I'm married. I told him I'm not going to go to lunch with him or go have a drink with him. He's asked me these things numerous times and I'm just really concerned. He shows up where I am, he's gotten to know a little bit about my schedule. He knows my phone number now. What do I do?"

I told Denise, "The best way to deal with a person who won't let go is for *you* to completely let go. Cease all communication with this individual. Don't respond to his calls. If he calls you ten times and you finally answer on the tenth time, what did you just teach him? That it takes ten calls to get you to answer. Stay away from those places where this person would be." She asked me what to do if that didn't work, and I told her eventually she might have to get the police involved, but I reiterated: "Your best intervention at this point is to completely let go, cease all communication, all contact with this individual." That's the best way to deal with that stalker, boyfriend, girlfriend, a person who is just pursuing you and they won't let up.

Most women I've talked to about this have faced a similar situation; a boyfriend, or wanna-be boyfriend, who wouldn't let up, who wouldn't let go. Unfortunately, in our society, there's that myth that persistence wins: "I finally convinced her to go out with me and now we're married." But today, you need to look at persistence in a different light. If someone tells you "no," respect that. If you're telling someone "no," be firm. Don't be wishy-washy. Say, "I don't want to go out with you. Leave me alone."

Anyone who is starting to become threatening in nature, is concerned about who you're with, doesn't want you to hang out with your friends, calls over and over, drives by your place of work or your home frequently—those are all flags of things that should alert you that this person is one that just might not let go.

Again, the best intervention for a person who won't let go—the stalker type individual—is that you completely let go at all cost. Don't send your older brother to go threaten this person; that tells the stalker that he or she is getting your attention, which is what they want. Let go. You're the one who lets go completely, 100%. You might have to get a restraining order, but there are some pros and cons to that as well, which are beyond the scope of this book. But completely let go.

Escape Plans if You're Taken Hostage

Until the events of September 11, 2001, we were taught, as a society, to submit to hijackers or hostage takers. We were taught that would keep us safe. That's simply not true.

In his book *Strong on Defense*, retired San Diego police officer Sanford Strong says never let an assailant get you to Crime Scene #2, because that's where he'll assault you, rape you, or kill you. Crime Scene #2 can be his car, it can be the place he wants you to drive to in your car—it's any-where other than the place you first encounter your assailant.

A police officer told me this story about Crime Scene #2:

> A 34-year-old professional woman met some friends for drinks in the downtown area of a medium-sized city. She owned a boutique just two blocks from the restaurant where they met, so she left alone to walk back to get her car. It's 11:30 at night, she's a woman alone, she'd been drinking, and she made the bad decision to take a shortcut through an alley to get to her car.
>
> A big white van pulled up behind her in this tight little space. She told me she could have run away, but she froze. A huge man grabbed her and tossed her in the van before she could even formulate a scream. He held her captive for six hours, raping her and beating her repeatedly. He even made her give him her PIN number for her debit card, drove to a convenience store, and left her in the van while he went inside to the ATM and got as much money as he could out of her account.
>
> She could have run away while he was in the store. She wasn't even tied up. She was just frozen in terror. Eventually, he dumped her out in a rural area. I think it's a miracle he didn't kill her. Luckily, that convenience store had a good camera with great resolution. The guy's in prison now, where he belongs.

So what could she have done? By now, you probably see a lot of places where this crime could have been prevented or at least ended earlier:

- Drinking impairs your awareness; she could have asked someone to walk with her to her car, or her friends could have been more vigilant and said, "You shouldn't walk alone."
- Taking the shortcut through that tight alley was a bad decision.

- If she'd played mental movies of possible abductions, she wouldn't have frozen. She would have trained her mind to run for it as soon as she sensed danger.

- If she'd practiced screaming "NO!" or "STOP!" she might have alerted someone that she needed help.

So let's say she'd done all those things, and this huge man simply overpowered her and forced her into the van, what then? This answer may surprise you: what you want to do then is force him to **crash the vehicle.**

If you're driving the vehicle, run into something—a pole, a guardrail, whatever. If your assailant is driving, grab the wheel suddenly and crash into a pole, a guardrail, a parked car, whatever. Is that going to alert people to a problem? Oh, absolutely. You stop the incident right there and you get help.

This victim had one more chance to escape: when she was sitting in the parked van in the convenience store parking lot. She could have run, but she was frozen in fear. Don't let fear rule you. Don't let it make you hyper-vigilant. Don't let it paralyze you when you need to act. Think about what you would do in different situations. Play those mental movies. Step into the OODA Loop, and figure out what you need to do *quickly* to get to safety.

Teach Your Children Well

Involve your children in creating your escape plans. Psychologists today tell you that kids as young as four years old (it depends on the individual child) are ready to be involved in the escape plan.

When I teach a class, I ask the all parents in the room a question: In the movie *Finding Nemo,* who are the bad guys? In that movie, the scuba divers, the sharks and the sea gulls are dangerous to all the little fish. Kids know that. They have a good understanding of bad guys and dangers. A friend with young children told me this story:

> I hadn't talked to my four-year-old daughter about "stranger danger" yet, because, honestly, she was young for four. She is a very sweet child, who sees the good

and beauty in everyone, and we just didn't know how to explain it to her at that point. But, we always told her, "Listen to your heart. That voice is God keeping you safe." It was an effective way to frame it for her, but I still worried that she was so sweet, if some creepy guy approached her, she wouldn't want to hurt his feelings.

One day, I was at the library with my daughter and my infant. We were in the foyer, and I was several paces ahead of my daughter. She was pre-occupied looking at the book she'd just checked out, and didn't realize a man was right behind her. Something about the guy made the hair on the back of my neck stand up. I couldn't tell you why, he just creeped me out. I didn't want to scare my daughter, so I said, in as even a tone as I could, "Come on, honey. Hurry up." She glanced up at me, noticed the creepy guy behind her, got wide-eyed and bolted for me. I'd never seen her react to anyone like that before. But it was very reassuring that she could sense if someone was potentially dangerous.

When you involve your kids in making escape plans, you don't want to create fear in them, so be cautious of your emotional state. Use a calm voice, and just be matter-of-fact. "This is what you're going to do, should something happen in our home." "If you're confronted out on the street, I want you to run with your mother to the [designated] safe zone. This is what you're going to do." You don't scare them, frighten them or infect them with your anxiety. Kids do fire drills at school all the time. It doesn't scare kids about a fire, it's part of training and readiness. Your leadership role when advising younger family members should be confident, and free of emotional fear. Just get them involved and share your plan with them.

Practice Your Escape Plans with Your Kids

Once in a while, maybe every three months, get everybody together and practice your escape plan. Go over it again verbally, then physically practice it. Yell your keyword (remember, in my family it's "intruder;" some friends of mine use "danger!' because their children are young, and can remember it better). Climb down that rope ladder. Jump out that first-floor window. Move through your house in the dark to get to your exit. Practice makes perfect.

Discuss other scenarios, especially upcoming events. "Here's what we're going to do when we're on vacation next month," talk about it real briefly over dinner. "Here's our plan and let's just kind of practice it, let's just play it out in our heads right now. Let's do that mental movie." Practice it in your mind's eye. It fills your mind with data and prepares you for the situation so that your mind, the amazing mind, can instantly go back to that data and you can act, you can do something right away. So you don't freeze up and end up a victim.

In elementary school, kids practice fire drills routinely, a few times a year, and it's coordinated. It's planned. There's a response. By junior high, they don't do it as much. By high school, they're already trained. They've already practiced. They know what to do when they hear the fire alarms.

When my kids were young, I started them practicing what to do if they were alone. So as the kids got old enough to where I could leave them alone from time to time, I knew they were safe in the house. I knew the doors were locked, I knew they wouldn't answer the door to a stranger, give away on the phone that they were alone in the house, and I knew they had a phone handy so they could call 911 in case something happens. (How many times have you hunted for your cordless phone? Make sure your kids have it handy before you leave the house. Make it a habit!)

I also started 911 drills when my kids were really young. I turned off the phone, or unplugged it, and had my daughters physically dial 911. We also had little sheets by the phone that had our address, parents' names and cell phone numbers, and any other pertinent information so that, when my child was stressed she could just read off that cheat sheet.

Unplug the phone, and give your kids a little scenario. Okay, here's what happened, what are you going to do? Have them pick up the phone and physically—that's the key, physically—dial 9-1-1. Then I'd ask my daughter, "Okay, now what? What would you tell the 911 operator?" Based on the scenario I've given them, they'd practice saying, "My sister has fallen, my parents are at the grocery store," etc.

That practice was important. When my older daughter, Kaley, was 16, she spent the night at her grandmother's house. Her grandma had gotten up in the middle of the night and tripped and fallen. She hurt her ankle and hit her head on the corner of the door. She had a big gash in her head, which was bleeding profusely.

She got a towel, put it on her head and kind of stumbled into the room where Kaley was sleeping and said, "Kaley, I think I need your help." Kaley saw the blood on the towel, realized that her grandma was hurt and said, "Grandma, I need to call 911." Her grandma said, "No, no. I'll be okay. Don't call." But Kaley was adamant and persistent, "Yes, I have to call 911, Grandma. You're injured." Over her grandmother's protests, Kaley called 911 and the paramedics showed up and took her grandmother to the hospital. It turned out she needed 17 stitches in her head, her ankle was fractured, she was pretty bruised-up, and they suspected she'd suffered a minor stroke. She spent two days in the hospital. It was a good thing Kaley "disobeyed" and called the paramedics!

A year later, Kaley was awarded the American Red Cross Humanitarian Award based on her safety skills. I truly believe she handled that situation so well because she had practiced it growing up, and knew what to do, and how to respond.

Right now, commit to look at all your environments and preplan your escape routes. Saying that you'll do it tomorrow, turns into someday, which turns into no follow-through. Be committed. You are the product of your habitual responses, so train your habitual responses.

Start in your inner circle and work your way out. Commit to developing an escape plan for your home, then your work place, then your vehicle, then public places you frequent. When you make that habitual, creating escape plans, every time you walk into a new restaurant, a different mall, a new grocery store, you'll automatically note where the exits are. It will become *habit*—not hyper-vigilance, not paranoia. It will be a habit that will help keep you safe.

The Active Shooter—Columbine, Virginia Tech, Fort Hood

The most extreme incident of violence in today's society is what is called the active shooter. This is the person who enters your home, work, school, public place, place of worship, etc. and opens fire on innocent people. I'm talking about Columbine, Virginia Tech, the mega-church in Colorado Springs, the shooting at Fort Hood. Sadly, it seems like not a month goes by that you don't hear about an incident where someone has opened fire, killing innocent men, women, and children.

Some people like to say that it's so unlikely you'll be in a situation like this, it'd be like getting hit by lightning. But it could happen. You know, you just could be at the wrong place at the wrong time and have to deal with an active shooter situation. And there are ways to survive an attack like that.

I think it's important to have some understanding of what an active shooter is likely to do, what his goals are, what his endgame might be. The current information and statistics on the active shooter are compiled based on real incidents that have happened in the last 10 years. What we know about the active shooter is:

- They are acting alone about 98% of the time, no other people or accomplices. Columbine was a rare exception.

- They are almost always male.

- About 90% of them are suicidal, and intend to commit suicide on-site, where they're committing this act of violence.

- They almost never take hostages, nor do they have any interest in negotiating.

- The active shooter is preoccupied with a high body count. It's a race against time, against the police, to kill as many people as they can. Seung-hui Cho, the shooter at Virginia Tech, killed 32 people and wounded many others.

- The active shooter carries multiple weapons and has the ability to reload his weapons several times. That means that he's going to have a fair amount of ammunition on him and the ability to reload or change magazines and to keep firing.

- Long arms, that is, rifles and shotguns, are involved most of the time. About 80% of the time the active shooter is going to use a shotgun or a rifle to commit his act of violence.

Most incidents with active shooters are over within four minutes or less. Four minutes. What's your police response time? It's impossible to predict; there could be a pile-up on a freeway, your town may not have

137

enough patrol officers, it could just be a busy day for misdemeanors. There's no way to know. It's very likely that the active shooter situation will be over before police come.

About half the time, the person stopping the incident is non-police; somebody who takes the initiative and does something to stop this violent act. Barry Dale Loukaitis, a 14-year-old in Moses Lake, Washington, who shot and killed a teacher and two students, and wounded another, was overpowered and subdued by gym coach Jon Lane.

But remember, 90% of active shooters are suicidal. Seung-hui Cho ended his own rampage at Virginia Tech by shooting himself in the head. With SWAT teams outside, Eric Harris and Dylan Klebold shot and killed themselves in the library of Columbine High School. You might have an opportunity to stop the active shooter and prevent more deaths, which we'll discuss below.

Surviving an Active Shooter Incident

1. Escape if safe to do so, as we've talked about over and over. If you can get away safely, do so. But if it's not safe, don't run out into the hallway, don't run out into the area where the potential violent person may be, making yourself a victim.

2. If you can't escape, hide and cover. Get under some real cover that will block bullets. Get to a safe room that protects you from incoming rounds. Cover is different from concealment; concealing yourself behind a curtain will not save your life. Bullets can go through concealment.

The Virginia Tech Massacre would have been much worse if students and teachers hadn't barricaded themselves in classrooms. Virginia State Police Superintendent William Flaherty told a state panel that police found 203 live rounds in Norris Hall. "He was well prepared to continue," Flaherty said.[8]

3. Once you're relatively safe, stay put and call 911. Provide as much information as you possibly can. The faster the police can respond and take out the shooter, the fewer people will die.

---

[8] "Va. Tech gunman had 200 more rounds to fire". MSNBC (Associated Press). 2007-05-21.

PLAN YOUR ESCAPE

During the Virginia Tech massacre, Professor Kevin Granata brought 20 students from a nearby classroom into an office, where the door could be locked. He went downstairs to investigate the noise and commotion, and was killed by Cho. But none of the students in the locked office were injured.[9] Another professor, Liviu Librescu, held his classroom door closed until most of his students escaped through the windows. Librescu died after being shot multiple times through the door, and one student in his classroom was killed, but he saved dozens more.[10]

So lock the doors in your immediate area. Make it much more difficult for the shooter to get in. Once you've locked those doors, if you can, place barriers up against the door as well. The shooter might shoot the lock, or shoot through the door, like Cho did. Get as much stuff against the doorway as you can—bookshelves, chairs, tables, anything to make it even harder for the active shooter to get in to your area.

4. As a last resort, you may need to attack the attacker. That's a tough one to think about, I know. But remember, active shooters usually stop to reload. Colin Ferguson killed 6 people and wounded another 19 on a commuter train in Long Island, NY, before he stopped to reload. That's when passengers Michael O'Connor, Kevin Blum and Mark McEntee tackled Ferguson and pinned him to one of the train's seats. Several other passengers ran forward to grab his arms and legs and help hold him down.[11]

That's a decision you'll have to make—one I hope you never have to make. But when faced with a situation where you can't escape and danger is imminent, are you going to stand there and become a victim or are you going to fight for your life? It's a decision only you can make.

5. The last point for surviving an active shooter is what to do when law enforcement arrives. It could take a while, but they eventually will arrive. If you're barricaded in a safe place because you couldn't escape, stay there until law enforcement arrives. You may hear a lull in the shootings, and

---

[9] Downey, Kirstin. "Loss Creates a Terrible Contrast in Lives So Similar". *Washington Post.* 2007-04-19.

[10] "Israeli lecturer died shielding Virginia Tech students from gunman". Haaretz. 2007-04-17.

[11] Schemo, Diana Jean (1993-12-09). "DEATH ON THE L.I.R.R.: The Confrontation; 3 Credited In Capture Of Gunman". *The New York Times.* Retrieved 2009-11-04.

most only last a few minutes, but Cho rampaged across the Virginia Tech campus longer, killing people in the dormitories before beginning his rampage through a classroom building. Stay put. When law enforcement arrives, go face down onto the ground, with your arms out to the side, and expose your hands palms up. The police are going to come in highly aggressive, looking for the shooter. The shooter may have committed suicide, but they won't know immediately, and they're looking for other potential shooters. Show them that you're not a threat by lying face down, palms up.

Your awareness and vigilance play the most important role in your overall prevention and intervention of violence. When faced with imminent danger, you must realize that mental strength will be absolutely necessary to stay alive and survive this type of situation.

What If?

Developing your escape plans takes commitment and practice—mental and physical. Playing the "what if" game helps you to develop escape plans.

As a security officer working in a medical center, I was frequently called back to the ER to do a "standby" outside a room where a potentially aggressive patient was—somebody under the influence, somebody with mental issues, someone that the nurse was concerned might become violent or try to flee. When I stood outside the room, I would run through the "what if's;" in my mind's eye, I would go through possible scenarios, and what I would do should something happen. What if the patient jumps up and bolts for the door? How will I contain them, control them? I'd play that out in my mind's eye. What if patient jumps up and grabs the IV pole, starts swinging it around, trying to strike people? How would I deal with that?

What if the patient grabs the nurse? Puts her in a headlock and pulls her to the ground? It's the when-then kind of thinking: when this happens, then I will do this. I was good at what I did because I had contingencies already in place. The best police officers, the best security officers, the best human resources personnel, the best Emergency Department nurses—the best of the best play the "what if " game, and they play it often.

In law enforcement, Field Training Officers (FTOs) train new recruits in police tactics. After police officers have gone through the academy and they're out in the real world, they still go through a training period for a number of months. The role of the FTO is to play the "what if " game with new police recruits, preparing them for the different situations that they're more than likely going to be involved in throughout their career. They know that preparing the mind is vital to surviving dangerous situations.

So "what if?" yourself. What if this happens at church on Sunday? What if I'm walking my dog and _____ happens? Don't "what if" yourself to death, just play that "what if" game for the different scenarios of different environments that you'll be in. It will help you build contingencies, in building data in your amazing, powerful mind, so that if something happens, you'll respond to that situation appropriately and automatically.

The One Thing You Can Be Sure of: Things Are Going to Change

The last thing I want to talk about when it comes to developing escape plans, surviving an active shooter, and "what iffing" is change. Realize now that things are going to change. You're going to change and so are most things in life. So doesn't it make sense to update your escape plans as your life changes? You know, as you get older, you don't move as well as you used to move, so that's a variable in my escape plan today. My kids are older and more able to handle themselves. I have a new vehicle now, so how do I get out of it or how do I get into it? Those are all part of the change in my escape plan. I travel more and more, so I need to be thinking about the changes now in my life in regards to that—how I'm going to escape from new environments, new areas that I'm in now that I wasn't before.

Realize that change is inevitable and be prepared. That's the Boy Scout motto and the American Red Cross motto: "be prepared." So be prepared in your escape planning, your response. Think through what you'll do, practice it in your mind, and physically practice. That will help you in any dangerous situation—foreseen or unforeseen.

.

"You are a product of your environment. So choose the environment that will best develop you toward your objective. Analyze your life in terms of its environment. Are the things around you helping you toward success—or are they holding you back?"

-W. Clement Stone, Successful American Entrepreneur and Best-Selling Author (1902-2002)

Chapter 9

Environmental Safety:
Be Safe Wherever You Are

How many environments are you in on a daily basis? Your home, your vehicle, the store, your work, wherever you went to lunch—several in any given day, right? Throughout this book you've learned how to increase your awareness and your vigilance, how to avoid danger, how to communicate with people. Those are all things you need to do in any environment that you're in to keep yourself safe.

Now, let's get down to brass tacks. In this chapter, you'll learn environmental safety tips. These are presented to give you a basic idea of how to keep yourself safe in different environments; but don't limit yourself to just these ideas on environmental safety factors. And remember, things are going to change, your environments are going to change. You must change to keep yourself safe in the different environments that you will be in throughout your life.

One note to men: don't think I'm only talking to women. Men get attacked, mugged, robbed, abducted or even raped, too. All of these safety tips apply to everyone.

Home

You spend a significant amount of your lifetime in your home. You sleep six to ten hours a night, you spend an hour or two getting ready for work in the morning, you come home for dinner, hang out on the weekend. You're in this environment a lot. What can you do right now to protect yourself and your family members in your home? How can you keep yourself safer while at home?

Lock Up! Lock your doors. After the Groene murders in Coeur d'Alene, investigators asked Joseph Edward Duncan, III, if there was anything the Groene's could have done to make themselves less of a target. His answer was chilling: they could have locked their back door. An acquaintance who worked on that investigation told me that Duncan entered through an unlocked back door.

Since the Groene murders, I developed the habit of walking through my front door and automatically locking it behind me. When I first start doing this, and it wasn't too long ago, it would drive my family crazy. I'd walk in, lock the door, they'd come home from the store, wherever, and they're beating on the door. I'd say, "Well, use your key. That's what it's for. The door's locked to keep others out. It's a safety thing." It's the simplest and most effective thing you can do to keep others out. Just lock your doors.

In my hometown in the late 1990s, juveniles were robbing houses during the day by simply walking up to the front door to see if it was locked. They'd knock to make sure no one was home, then try the door if no one answered. They'd walk right in to unlocked houses and steal small items before neighbors or anyone noticed anything amiss. Burglars don't knock on the door, right?

Specifically, use deadbolt locks on all exterior doors. Consult a locksmith if needed. A small chain between the door and the door jam is not necessarily safe. It can be easily broken or ripped out. Install solid core doors, too. They'll hold up against an assault much better.

Before moving into a new residence or a rental, have the locks changed. Who knows how many keys are floating around out there from previous tenants, or their friends or relatives?

Lock your windows, too. They're another potentially easy access point for would-be criminals. If you leave a window open for ventilation, keep the opening small enough to prevent entry. Use window locks and dowels. Check that the windows are locked before retiring at night. Make that a habit, if you haven't already—check the entrances and the windows right before going to bed.

Lock your exterior buildings, too. Keep your garages and any other exterior sheds or buildings locked. Design or redesign your fences and gates to open only from the inside of your property.

Lights On. Criminals don't like lights. Good exterior lighting on the outside of your home can discourage prowling or loitering. I keep my outside light on 24/7/365. I pay a little extra money every year to keep that light on, but it sends a message that I plan to be aware of who is around my house.

Install outside lights on all entryways, pathways, stairwells, trash and parking areas. Consider connecting outside lights to a timing device, motion detector or light-sensitive switch so lights switch on automatically during hours of darkness.

In Your Home. When you're home, close the shades, blinds or curtains, especially at night. If someone is outside in the darkness, and you're in a well-lit house with no shades or curtains, they can see your every move. You can be observed and stalked without even knowing it.

Leave lights on in two or more rooms to indicate the presence of other people.Never open doors to strangers. If a visitor identifies himself as a police officer or a service person, obtain their badge number and/or ID and have them wait while you call to verify this.

Install wide-angled viewers (peepholes) in the doors at all entrances so you can see who is outside without opening the door. Look through the viewer before opening the door! My front door has arching windows at the very top of the door, so even I have to stand on my tiptoes to see who's out there (I'm six feet tall). I can also go to the front window to see who's standing at the doorway. If you're short, have one installed at your eye-height. Having two viewers in your door is better than having one useless one because you can't see out of it.

Post Your House Number Clearly. Your house or apartment number should be well lit and properly exposed for emergency vehicles to identify. If you need to call the police, fire department, or emergency personnel, they need to be able to spot your home so they can help you.

Come Home Safely. When you approach your house, approach it safely. When arriving home, be on the guard when entering and approaching entrances. Your keys and your cell phone should be in hand or within reach at night. Keep your car lights on and the car doors locked until you have checked your garage or parking area. Look around before you get out of your car. Be aware.

If you're driven home, ask your driver—whether it's a friend or a cab driver—to wait until you're safely inside your residence. If at all possible, arrange for a friend, relative or neighbor to be there when you arrive at home if by chance you might be coming home to an empty house.

If you come home and find the door or window open, or signs of forced entry, do not go in. Let me say that again—do not go in. Go to a trusted neighbor and call the police. If you're at home and you suspect someone is trying to break in, dial 911 immediately.

If confronted by an intruder in your home, your best plan is to escape. You have an escape plan now, right? Right? If not, review Chapter 8!

CPTED—Crime Prevention through Environmental Design, or CPTED, became very popular in the 1980s. It's a concept that most businesses employ when designing new buildings. It takes into account exterior landscaping, lighting, entrances and exits, etc., so that predators don't have places to hide.

CPTED concepts can help you evaluate and correct vulnerable areas outside of your home. For instance, consider removing and trimming shrubs or foliage that can provide a hiding area for a criminal. Google search "Crime Prevention through Environmental Design" to give you some ideas of what businesses are doing to prevent crime to their businesses, so you can design your business or home by doing some landscaping to prevent those hiding places.

Neighbors. Neighbors are your number one safety mechanism—after keeping your house locked. Your neighbors can be the best security system. They can alert you of suspicious activities, watch your home when you're away, collect your paper or mail, and put your trash out, so it looks like you're still there even though you're away. I always let my next door neighbors know when I'm going to be out of town, what dates I'll be gone, and when I'm coming home. They have my cell number if they need to contact me. We've made that pact that we're going to watch out for each other, so I do the same for them when they're out of town.

Contact neighbors whenever a crime or a theft occurs so that they can take appropriate precautions themselves and keep an eye out for suspicious activity.

Neighborhood watch programs have been essential in reducing burglaries, by as much as 45% in some areas. Get involved or start your own neighborhood watch program. Neighbors working together in cooperation with law enforcement make one of the best crime fighting deterrents. Report any suspicious activity whatsoever immediately to the local police.

The Broken Window Theory. The broken window theory states that a successful strategy for preventing vandalism, petty crime, low-level anti-social behavior and even major crimes, is to fix a neighborhood's problems when they are small. This is a theory tested and evaluated all over the world: New York City; the Netherlands; Lowell, Massachusetts; and Albuquerque, New Mexico, to name a few.

What that means is repair broken windows within a short time, say a day or a week. Then vandals are much less likely to break more windows or to do further damage.

As a parent, I've seen this at work in my kids' rooms: I make them clean their room, and it stays cleaner. Once they slip and the room's a mess again, dirty clothes never make it to the hamper, books get strewn about rather than stacked neatly. Think about it, and I'm sure you'll see examples of this in your own home. A cleared off table stays cleared. Once it's cluttered up, the clutter seems to multiply on its own.

So report broken street lights to city or utility agencies immediately. Clean up your sidewalks every day; don't let litter accumulate, and the rate of littering will be much less. If your neighborhood says "well-tended" to a criminal, it might also be saying, "you're being watched."

Mark Your Property. Even with your best efforts, there's still the possibility you'll get robbed. So engrave your valuable property. Keep a record of serial numbers and valuable equipment. Photograph or videotape other valuables. Keep photographs, videotapes and records of serial numbers separate from your valuables in a safe or safety deposit box. In that way if you do have a burglary, a crime, a theft and the police do potentially get your valuables back, now you can identify them. If you can't identify them, you might not get them back.

Guard Animals. Dogs can offer an additional home protection for you. Selection factors should include the type of dog, the training of the dog, obviously your location, and the feasibility of having a dog. It's something to think about, especially if you're living alone. You might want to get a dog for that extra protection and companionship. But do some research. Find out what kind of dog is going to work best for you, your family, and your home.

Safety Surveys. Many law enforcement agencies offer free home security surveys that can provide specific recommendations for your residence. Contact your local agency and request their assistance.

What are some additional steps that you can take to keep yourself and your family safe in your home? I want you to think about that for just a moment here. What is unique about your home that makes it inherently safe—or less safe?

Advanced Home Safety Precautions

Most of these advanced home safety measures are going to cost some money. You need to decide if they're needed in your neighborhood. I just want you to have a basic understanding of some advanced home security systems that you can put in place.

Alarm Systems

I'm sure you've seen little placards or signs in front yards that say, "Protected by _____ Alarm Company". That announcement of a security system in place is a powerful deterrent to predators and criminals. Remember— they're looking for easy prey. But systems are only as good as the people using them, so you need to remember that. Learn how to use your security system properly.

Audible alarms alert and draw attention. Criminals are distracted by loud noises, just like we are. A loud alarm can be a good deterrent to a thief or predator.

Monitored alarms send a signal to a remote location alerting them to a breach in your security. Monitoring doesn't necessarily mean you will have an immediate response to your alarm.

Contact a reputable licensed alarm company and get references. Talk to some people who use these types of systems in their homes. Investigate the pros and cons of having a monitored alarm system. If you're getting false alarms and the police are showing up or a security agency is showing up, they're going to charge you.

Motion detectors are sensors that pick up movement. They can be connected to lighting, so if the detector senses a movement, a light will come on. They can also be connected to cameras, so the camera will turn in that direction and start recording, as well as setting off an audible alarm. They can also be monitored by a security company.

Motion detectors are often placed in windows, window areas, and door areas; places where somebody might try to gain entry.

Floodlights are great. They put out a tremendous amount of light when triggered, which deters criminals. Floodlights can be used in conjunction with motion sensors, cameras and audible alarms.

Cameras and CCTV

CCTV stands for Closed Circuit Television. CCTV cameras transmit to a specific place, such as a control room. Video cameras can allow you to see what is happening in different areas of your home when you are not there. If you do have a bigger home and a gated entrance with an intercom, you can look at the monitor and see who is trying to enter through your gate.

Security cameras are expensive, so contact a reputable licensed security installation company and get references. Costco offers an affordable system with four cameras that record to a DVR (digital video recording device).

Video is mostly used after the fact, for an investigation. Seldom does it get used as a preventative measure, unless somebody is actually sitting there and watching the monitor.

Tinted Windows

Tinted windows make it easy to see out of windows and hard for people to see in. It's very common in business and commercial settings, and you might consider doing that in your home.

Safe Rooms

A safe room or a panic room is a secured room that separates the homeowner from intruders, providing a safe place to await the arrival of police or security personnel. In my next home, I plan to install a safe room. You can put valuables in a safe room, but primarily it's a place that you and your family can go should you have a home invasion.

Secured Lines

Communication and power lines or boxes can be easily cut or disabled if not secured properly. Most outside alarm monitoring is signaled via your phone lines, so if you invest in an alarm system, get a secured line. Safe rooms should have a secure phone line installed so you can call for help or hit a panic button that alerts police. Contact the appropriate utility company before making any changes to your power or your phone lines.

Security Patrols

There are many security companies today that offer security patrols of residences and businesses. Some neighborhood associations contract for security patrols, too. If you're considering this, contact a reputable licensed security company and get references.

People at Your Door

Picture this: you're sitting home one evening, alone, your family or your significant other is away, and you're just at home alone, enjoying a quiet evening. Suddenly, you hear a knock at the door, or the doorbell. You're not expecting anybody. You look through your peephole, and it's someone you don't know. Would you answer the door?

ENVIRONMENTAL SAFETY: BE SAFE WHEREVER YOU ARE

Don't Answer the Door to Strangers

If an unknown person is at your door, never let them know that you're alone. And never open your door to someone you don't know. Just never do it. Just make a stance on that right now that you're just not going to do that. Educate all family members on this safety rule as well. It's not paranoia, it's vigilance.

Talk through the door if you need to. Identify the person. Absolutely do NOT open the door to anyone without first verifying the person's identity. This includes police officers, repairmen, delivery or sales persons, and political or charity volunteers. Again, use that wide-angle door viewer, or look through the curtains or blinds to see who is at your door.

Ask to see the identification and have the person slip their identification under the door. If you have any doubts about the person, look up the telephone number in the telephone directory and call the company or agency the person claims to be from, even police officers. Police, especially, should validate you that you're taking the appropriate safety precautions. You don't have to open your door to anybody. This is your right. So it's just important to remember that and to understand it and practice it.

Solicitors

Consider posting a "no soliciting" sign. That's going to keep unknown people from just walking up and knocking on your door.

Can I Use Your Phone?

If an unknown person is requesting help or to use your telephone, offer to make the call for them while they wait outside. You're talking to them through the door, get the telephone number and say, "I will call for help for you." If they legitimately need help, they'll wait. If they were trying to gain entry to rob or attack you, they'll leave.

Packaged Deliveries

Have parcels left outside your door. Required signature receipts can be slipped under the door. I know my regular UPS guys, so I'm not concerned about them, but if you're not familiar with the delivery people in your area, just have parcels left on your steps. They can be picked up once you're sure the delivery person has driven away.

Train your family. Train the people around you. Your children should be trained to never answer the door. Just never answer it. Again, trust your instincts. If something doesn't seem right, it probably isn't. Be vigilant to stay safe.

Telephone Safety

Thanks to Caller ID, Call Blocking, and Do Not Call lists, we have a lot less annoying phone communication these days, don't we? But technology changes so fast, it's hard to keep up with all the phone scams out there. Elderly folks, in particular, get solicited and scammed over the phone, and people can lose a lot of money that way. These standard practices for phone safety will help protect you and your family. Again, make sure you teach these to your children, too.

- Limit the information that you give out over the phone. Do not give out any personal information to callers seeking information about you for a survey, a credit check or a subscription drive. Call the agency or company the person works for and verify the identity and intent of the telephone call.

- If you get a "wrong number" call, do not give your phone number to the caller; ask "What number are you trying to call?" Never reveal your address or that you're home alone.

- List only your first initial and last name in the telephone directory. Do not list your address.

- Consider restricting your number. You'll show up on Caller ID as "Restricted" or "Unknown Caller."

- Enroll in the "do not call" directories. You can Google that to find out those numbers and get taken off those lists.

I might come across as rude sometimes when I get calls soliciting for charity groups. I'm not anti-charity, I give to charity, but calling me on the telephone is invasive, in my opinion. I'll hang up immediately or I'll say,

"Mail me some information." If they got my phone number legitimately, they can get my address legitimately.

Threatening Calls

If you receive a threatening, harassing or obscene telephone call, notify the police and your telephone company. When you receive these calls, immediately put the phone down—don't hang up—and don't say anything. If it's continual, keep filing police reports so they can track them and find out who's doing it. Keep records of the dates and times of the calls, and the content of each telephone call for the police and telephone company. You can have these calls blocked by your cell provider, too.

Of course, if the calls are from a stalker, he or she will call you from another telephone. Remember with stalkers, even though they won't let go, you let go completely. Don't respond; don't react.

Practice Emergency Calls

I shared with you earlier in the book how I trained my two daughters to call 911. But it's important for adults to rehearse those calls, too. A stress level response can inhibit you from making calls. Your fingers just don't quite work as well when you're stressed, when your heart rate is real high. But if you've conditioned yourself, you automatically go to that.

Practice these phone calls and remember the relevant and the appropriate information that you're going to give to the dispatchers. Have that sheet handy with your address. I've worked with a couple of different 911 call centers, and they're excellent. They practice and are trained in what to ask you.

My friend Ray has taught emergency first aid for years. He knows all these things, but when his wife of forty years collapsed in front of him, his mind went blank; he literally couldn't remember his own address, a home he'd lived in for decades. Fortunately, his son was there and made the 911 call while Ray gave his wife CPR. The stress of seeing his wife collapse was just too much for even a professional, so post that information at your phones for these emergencies that can happen.

Cell Phones Are a Safety Tool

In all my classes, I ask everyone to raise their hand if they have a cell phone. I've only had maybe a dozen people who don't carry one. Everyone looks at that person in surprise. Usually the response is, "Well, I can't afford it right now," "It's broken," or "I lost it." Most people want and use a cell phone.

Very occasionally, someone says they have a moral objection to cell phones. Unfortunately, those people are robbing themselves of a vital safety tool. Would you drive around without a spare tire? That's a reasonable safety precaution. So is having a cell phone. If you don't want to pay for a phone, get a pre-paid with minutes that never expire. Don't give the number out, so people can't call you. You may never use it, but you'll have it if you need it.

Your cell phone is an emergency safety device, and a notification device. Use it to its full capacity.

Start with your emergency numbers. Program your phone with ICE numbers. "ICE" stands for "In Case of Emergency." When you enter your spouse, child, parent, significant other, whomever, as an emergency contact, enter them like this: [space] ICE Name, [relationship]. The space in front of ICE ensures that it appears at the top of your alphabetical list of contacts. So my daughter appears this way: "[Space] ICE 2 Kaley, daughter." (ICE 1 is Genelle, spouse.) If emergency personnel need to contact someone for me, they will find the contact name quickly in my phone.

People have used their cell phones to get help without even alerting the predator that they're calling. You can dial 911 and not put the phone near your ear. Shouting out "NO!" or "STOP!" and your location is a distraction to the assailant, and will alert the dispatcher that you need help.

Vacation Safety for Your Home

Do you worry about your house when you're away? I know I do. When I go on vacation, I take some preventative measures so that my home is safe while I'm gone. That way, I can enjoy my vacation and focus on relaxing, not worrying that my house is getting ransacked. The rules for vacation home safety are simple:

- Lock all your doors, windows, sheds and garages. Lock up. Lock everything up.

- Notify someone that you'll be gone.

- Have someone you trust pick up your mail, your newspapers, or you can even temporarily stop your mail and the newspaper.

- Leave a vehicle or two there, if possible, so it looks like someone is there all the time. That may mean getting a ride to and from the airport.

- Give emergency contact numbers to a relative or trusted neighbor. Check in with them so your whereabouts are always known and they have a way to contact you should something happen.

My neighbors get the newspaper, pick up the mail for us, and feed the cats. They have a key to the garage so they can get in to feed the cats, and they pull the garbage container out on Friday when the garbage comes, so our house doesn't look vacant. When they go out of town, I do the same thing for them.

Those are the basic guidelines to keep your house safe when you're away. There are some other precautions you can consider, too.

Timers and alarms. Use timing devices to turn on inside and outside lights and radios to give the appearance that your residence is occupied. Set timers to go on and off at different hours and in different rooms. Timing devices can activate alarms to be set at different times.

Be particularly vigilant around the holidays. Holidays are a typical time when predators seek opportunities to burglarize a house.

Leave your home looking as though things are perfectly normal. Your lawn is mowed, your trash picked up, newspapers and mail are not stacking up outside your front door. If you're going on an extended vacation, you might hire some kid down the street to mow your yard while you're gone.

Tell the police you're leaving. Some police departments will do periodic checks if you inform them you'll be gone. Not all of them, but they might have a verification check program. Tell them the dates you will be away and request that they periodically check your house. Most agencies don't have the manpower to provide this service, but it's worth checking into.

What else can you do to keep your home safe when you're away? I want you to think about what is unique about your home or your situation that protects your home—or might make it a target?

Being Safe with Your House and Car Keys

Make duplicates. Give a copy of your house key to a relative, a trusted friend, or a neighbor in case you ever get locked out.

"Hidden keys" are not necessarily hard to find. Do not put your key under the flowerpot, under the doormat, in a mailbox, on top of the door jamb, or any other places they might be easily found.

There are little combination lockboxes that you can hide, but be careful, because those can be broken into. One hard hit with a hammer will open that little lockbox, and now a predator has your house key.

If you're going to use an outside lockbox or fake rock with a hidden compartment for a house key, I recommend that you hide it really, really well. Make it hard for somebody to find that lockbox.

Never, never ever place any type of personal identification on your key rings. If you lose your keys, you do NOT want a predator to have your address and a key to your house and your car. Make sure you can separate your car key from all your other keys when you leave your car with a valet or you have it serviced or repaired. Do not leave all your keys on your keychain when not on your person.

Think about this, ladies. You drop your car off to get serviced, and you leave your whole key chain, because it'll only be an hour, and you're walking down the block for lunch. An hour is plenty of time for a dishonest employee to make a copy. Now he or she has your address and a key to your house. Not safe. Not smart. Not vigilant. Separate your keys, and only give your car key to anyone servicing or parking your car.

Lost keys = change your locks. If you ever lose your keys to your home, change the lock as soon as possible. It's pretty cheap. You go to Lowe's or Home Depot and buy those replacement kits. I'm not a handyman, but I can change those at least, and I think most of us can. It's not worth the risk.

Keep your keys ready. Before I get out of my car, my house key is between my index finger and my thumb, ready to go into the door. When I walk out of my house, my car key is between my index finger and my thumb, ready to use.

Have you ever got to your front door at night, maybe you forgot to turn on the outside lights? Now you're fumbling around with your keys, because you can't see very well. Now you're standing in the dark, distracted, fumbling with your keys. Are you aware? Are you vigilant? Could you avoid someone who came at you? Could you defend yourself? Escape?

Your key should be in your hand, ready to go when you get to that door lock, so you can safely and quickly get into your home, your car, your office, wherever.

Keys can be effective distractions and defense weapons. You can use your keys and your keychain holders to swing at the face of an aggressor, causing a distraction. Keys can also be used as an impact device to defend yourself. The level of civilian defense applies in all self-defense situations. You want to remember that—use reasonable force.

My keychain holder is what's called a Kubotan. It's a small dowel, about the size of a marker pen that was developed by Master Kubota. I like it because I can use it as a handle to swing the keys around, as a distraction towards the face of an aggressor.

When I put my keys on the ring, I specifically alternate the direction of the key edges, so every other one is facing the same way. That way, if I have to use my keys to defend myself, I swing them at the aggressor's face. With the teeth of the keys alternating, I can be reasonably certain that those keys are going to impact some flesh, the sharp part of them.

The key holder itself, the Kubotan, can also be used as an impact weapon, but that requires some training.

Again, you need to fully understand "reasonable force," and the other legal definitions we talked about in Chapter 5.

Vehicle Safety

Vehicle safety is about more than getting in, getting out, and driving carefully. There are a lot of things to consider when it comes to your vehicle environment.

What's in Your Vehicle?

While I was working at the medical center in security services, we had a rash of vehicle break-ins. The thieves would smash the window, steal the stereo or any belongings or valuables—then grab the vehicle registration. Why? It had the home address on it. The thief knew the car owner was at work, so they went to people's homes and robbed them. If they got a hold of the garage door opener, they got right in the house, or at least they could break into the house from the privacy of the garage.

Since then, I've started carrying my registration in my wallet. I recommend people take their garage door openers with them. At the very least, lock those items in the glove box.

There are certain things that should be in your vehicle, though:

- Local maps or GPS
- Flashlight
- Jumper cables
- Emergency tire inflation cans
- Flares
- First aid kit
- And of course, your cell phone. Keep it handy, too. If you need to call for help, having it buried in your purse or briefcase is not very helpful.
- GAS! Don't drive on empty. You don't want to run out of gas in a dangerous area. Consider installing locking gas caps, if fuel theft is a problem in your area.

ENVIRONMENTAL SAFETY: BE SAFE WHEREVER YOU ARE

Stay Alert

Don't let yourself be distracted while driving. Resist applying cosmetics, reading (people have caused accidents because they had a book in their lap!), texting, or making or taking calls on your cell phone.

Even hands-free phones are no safer than hand-held ones. In fact, they're so distracting, in studies drivers talking on cell phones drove worse than drunk drivers! And practice doesn't make perfect. People claim they get used to driving and talking, but studies show no improvement over time. So stay off your phone when you're driving![12]

Those are distractions that take you away from being in the moment. We've all gotten complacent, and we forget we're driving two tons of metal at 70 miles per hour. Pay attention. Stay safe.

Know where you are. Know your location. Be careful not to drive into areas of known crime activity. Plan your route in advance, particularly on unfamiliar trips. So it's nice to have maps and GPS.

Get fuel at trusted establishments that are safe, well lit, and attended. If you're in an unknown city, be aware and trust your instincts. One of my friends drives into new gas stations, sits for a minute, and looks around. If she feels unsafe, she just drives off.

While in Your Car

Always keep your doors locked. Predators have hopped into cars while people were stopped at red lights and stop signs.

Keep your windows up. Predators can reach in and grab you, your child, or reach in to unlock the door. If you're renting a car, make sure it has air conditioning so that you can keep those windows up.

You've heard this before, but never, ever pick up hitchhikers. Do I need to tell you why?

If another motorist is in trouble, don't stop, call for help. You can alert them, signal them with your hand that you're calling for help and further assistance. Some predators will fake car trouble to get someone to stop.

---

[12] Melissa Healy, "Hands-free cellphone use while driving won't make the roads safer, studies show. Why? Brain overload." *Los Angeles Times*, 2008.06.30

Wear your seatbelts. They save thousands of people every single year. You're not safe unless you're wearing yours. I grew up without a seatbelt and it was a tough habit to get into, but now I have the habit. My kids don't even think about it, though; buckling up has been habitual for them their whole lives. Fortunately, my car has an alarm to remind me if I forget. Nothing more irritating than that chime going off.

Keep your wallet, purse and other valuables out of sight while driving. Do not leave them on the seat next to you. Some aggressive thieves will "smash and grab" at stop signs or red lights, grab your purse, laptop, or briefcase, and be off and running before you can even get your seatbelt off. Place your personal items in the glove compartment, under a front seat or in the trunk. Do not store valuable items in your car.

Breakdowns

Reduce the chance of a breakdown by keeping your vehicle maintained and full of gas. If you do breakdown, get on your cell phone and call for help immediately. If it's safe to get out of your vehicle, open the hood to signal you're broken down. You can also attach a white handkerchief or some type of a cloth to the side mirror. Turn on your hazard lights.

Obviously, you're going to need to use some common sense, depending on your situation. If it feels safe to you, and you need to change a flat, do it. But if it's night, or if you're alone, stay in the car with the doors locked and the windows closed.

If someone stops and offers you help, do not get out of the car. Never leave with the person to seek help. Ask the person to help by calling the police or a towing service.

If the person makes you at all uncomfortable, LIE. Tell them the tow truck driver, your friend, spouse, relative, or even the police are only minutes away. Dial your phone as they are walking up to you, and give whomever you are talking to a description of the person. Give them the license plate of the car, if you can see it. TRUST YOUR INSTINCTS!

Accidents

Some criminals intentionally hit your car so they can carjack you, rob you, or worse. It's a ploy serial rapists have used to trap a victim—bump a woman's car, then grab her when they pull over to exchange information. Be cautious; don't get out of your car unless you absolutely need to. Call the police immediately so you don't get involved in those bump-and-rob situations or carjacking. Once the police get there, then get out and exchange information.

If it's very minor, signal the other driver to follow you to the nearest police station, sheriff or state patrol department to report the incident. Or go to a busy, well-lit parking area. No need to get out and inspect the damage if your vehicle will still move. You can do that when you're in a safe zone.

Road Rage

If an aggressive driver is following you, they're threatening you. Maybe you've cut them off inadvertently, so they're coming after you. But who knows what they want to do? Maybe they want to verbally harass you. Maybe they want to physically assault you.

I've had numerous people share road rage stories with me. They usually go something like this, "I cut him off—I didn't mean to, obviously—but the guy honked and followed me." "So what did you do?" I'll ask. "Well, I went home," they'll answer. Wrong thing to do! Now the aggressor knows where you live. If you suspect you're being followed, don't go home. Go to the police station. Go to the fire station. Go somewhere that's safe. If you have a GPS, you can find those safe zones quickly and easily. Flash your lights, honk your horn. Those are distractions that will alert others to your potentially dangerous situation.

Do not exit your car until you're at a safe location. Know where those police departments are. Know where the fire department is. Call the police—even if you're driving—if you feel threatened. Trust your instincts.

Alarm Systems

Consider installing an alarm system in your car. Many have a remote device that unlocks the car and turns on the interior lights. Women, especially, know to check their back seats before they get in their car, but the automatic interior lights are an excellent aid. Remember to use that fob to lock the doors immediately, too, as soon as you're in your car. That loud car alarm can come in handy. A woman in one of my classes told me this story:

> My garage is under my house, and one night I thought I heard somebody trying to break into my house through my garage. I had my car keys right next to my bed, so I hit the alarm button on my key fob. The alarm must have been deafening in the enclosed garage. But I didn't hear any more noise after that.

I would suggest that she should have called the police, anyway. The predator could have been lurking outside, could have tried another house, any number of scenarios.

Too many people leave exterior garage doors unlocked, which makes the interior garage door to the house an easy target for a thief. They have plenty of time and cover to break in through that door. Consider arming your car alarm even when it's parked in the garage. If an intruder bumps it, they'll set off the alarm. And if they're trying to steal your car out of your garage, they're not going to have a quiet getaway.

Public Transit Safety

On buses, trains, or subways, there are some basic safety precautions that you should be aware of. People who use them regularly can get too comfortable, and people using them as tourists can be too visible as targets. Follow these basic guidelines.

- Increase your awareness. If you're on a plane, your fellow passengers have been pre-screened. But anyone can hop on a bus, train or subway. Don't lose yourself in a book, don't blare your music in your iPod so loudly you can't hear what's going on around you, don't veg out, don't fall asleep. People are constantly getting on and getting off—be aware of who is around you. Be alert to who gets on and off the train or bus with you. Pay attention.

- If someone gets on your train, bus or subway train who makes you nervous, change compartments if you can, or get off at the next stop. Trust your instincts. You can grab the next one.

- If possible, do not wait alone at a bus stop, a train station or a taxi cab stand. Locate convenient, well-lighted, frequently used bus stops, train stations, and taxi cabs. Stand with other people or near the token information booth. Safety in numbers.

- Always check public transportation schedules prior to arriving. Know what you're going to do, where you're going to go, and how you're going to get there—especially if traveling at odd hours. Know where you're going and how to get back.

- If you can, sit near the driver. Avoid sitting near an exit door. An attacker can reach in and grab a purse, briefcase or jewelry.

- If you are harassed, report the incident to the driver immediately. Try to get off as soon as you can. If you feel you are being followed, inform other passengers getting off with you or walk to a place where there are other people who can assist you. Report any and all incidents to the police or security personnel immediately.

Safety in Parking Lots and Parking Garages

Parking lots are risky areas, especially at night. People get abducted, assaulted, mugged and carjacked in parking lots. These are some simple, even obvious, parking lot safety guidelines. Don't be complacent. Use these precautions. Always be aware of your surroundings in parking lots or garages; be aware and be vigilant.

- Always park in well-lit areas.

- Do not park near shrubs or other potential hiding areas.

- Get a security escort. Especially at odd hours, when the parking garage or parking lot is deserted. Even shopping malls have security personnel, and it's their job.

- Use a buddy system. Always walk in groups when possible—there's safety in numbers.

- When approaching your vehicle, look around for loiterers before you get into or near your car. If you're walking out to the parking garage and you see trouble, turn around, walk back into the mall, store, or workplace and get help.

- Have your keys ready in hand as you approach your vehicle.

- Have your cell phone handy.

- Know your location when calling for help.

- Report suspicious activity to security or police—but go to a safe public place to call for help.

- Keep your valuables and packages locked in your trunk. If you're carrying packages, try to keep one hand free, even if it means making an extra trip.

- Don't loiter in the parking lot. Don't sit around in the car making calls, checking email, or balancing your checkbook.

- Always turn off the ignition. Remove the key and lock your doors no matter how soon you plan on returning.

- Walk in the center aisle rather than close to parked cars, especially in parking garages. This will give you time and distance if someone tries to assault, rob or abduct you.

- Do not park next to vans, trucks with campers or other vehicles whose size and structure can provide concealment for a potential assailant—or that a predator could easily pull you into. If you return to your car, and see that there is now a van or a camper parked next to your vehicle that looks suspicious, or gives you an odd feeling, walk back into the store. Get a security escort. Wait for help. Better to be safe than to be sorry.

- Choose parking areas that have an attendant if possible.

- Choose locations that have heavy pedestrian traffic.

- Be aware of occupied cars around you. If someone is loitering in the parking lot, why? If you're uncomfortable, go back into the store.

- If you return to your car and find it disabled, go back in to the store to call for help. Criminals have been known to disable a car by flattening a tire to strand their victim. The victim is then approached, offered assistance and attacked. If a stranger appears and offers to help you, escape the area, scream loud and long, and report to police immediately.

ATMs

Since I am an advocate of avoidance, I generally suggest avoiding standalone Automated Teller Machines, or ATMs. But they're so convenient. I can stop off at an ATM anytime if I need some cash. I can make deposits, check my balance, transfer money around. Very convenient. Still, I recommend doing as much on-line as you can, and getting cash back during regular banking hours. But there are some reasonable precautions to take if you are going to use an ATM.

- Don't carry your PIN anywhere on your person or in your wallet, and never give your PIN to anyone. In Mexico, the last four or five years, it's been very popular for criminals to abduct people for their ATM card and their number. They'll take you somewhere, get the card and PIN number from you and get that $300, $400 or $500 that they can get in one shot.
- Have your paperwork and ATM card ready before you arrive at the ATM, so you can finish your transaction as quickly as possible.
- When you're done, secure your money in your pocket, wallet or purse before you even turn away from the ATM, and take the receipt with you.
- Hide your PIN when you're entering it. So if I'm standing there in front of the ATM, I want to shield the screen so that another person doesn't see me entering my pin. Same thing with my debit card at the grocery store, I always just kind of blade my body so the person behind me can't see me punching the number into the debit machine. Some criminals were using their phones to photograph or video people entering their PINs, then mugging them in the parking lot. A person thinks they've just lost their wallet, but the thief now has the ability to get several hundred dollars out of their bank account immediately.
- Be aware of your surroundings. Be aware of the people around the ATM and in parked cars who seem to be loitering or subtly watching customers transact business. If you feel uncomfortable, leave

the location; find another ATM where you can safely transact your business.

- If people are using an ATM when you arrive, avoid standing right behind them. Give them enough space to conduct their transaction in privacy.
- Report suspicious activity or persons to bank personnel and the police immediately.
- When using a drive-up ATM, be sure your car doors are locked and the windows are closed as you drive up. Look around and check the area before you open your car window to make sure no one is loitering around the ATM.
- Don't wait around. Once you've used the ATM, get out of the area. You probably have some cash on you now, so don't sit in your car or at the ATM and do your personal accounting.
- Make sure the ATM is not obscured by landscaping or walls. You want a clear view of it as you approach it. Secured ATMs in bank foyers seem safe, but all a criminal has to do is steal an ATM card from that bank and swipe it to get inside the ATM foyer. You don't always need a pin to enter the ATM foyer. Sometimes they lay in wait in the foyer, sometimes they follow you in.
- If at all possible, never use an ATM after dark. I have a friend who will go to the grocery store and buy gum to get $100 back, if she needs to. She doesn't use the grocery store as a bank, but in a pinch it's safer than using an ATM at night.
- Use inside ATMs whenever possible. Choose locations with lots of people around—in shopping malls, the market, or an ATM that is in a bank or located near a busy street. So find an ATM in a busy, well-lit, safe place.

Walking, Running and Biking Safety

Remember that lakeside hill I like to run and hike on? It's absolutely beautiful, but it's very secluded, and there have been assaults there and, many years ago, even a couple of rapes. Yet I still see women walking around the hill *alone*. People are more aware, and it's gotten safer, but that's a basic precaution for being outdoors—particularly for women, and younger girls or boys—have a buddy. Safety in numbers. I do run alone there, but only during busy hours. I'm also a black belt and defensive tactics expert. But none of that negates what would be my first defense: escape. If someone tried to attack me, I'd run away!

There are other safety guidelines, too. Think about these, and think about specific things that might apply to your routine, your neighborhood, or your physical abilities as you walk, run, hike, bike, or do whatever it is that you love to do outdoors. These guidelines are not just for outdoor recreation, however. They also apply to you if you live in an area where you mostly walk to get around town to and from work, to the stores, to restaurants, whatever.

- Avoid running, biking or walking at night. It's just not safe. Aside from the physical dangers of being hit by a car, falling and hurting yourself, and being stuck outside, you're just a much easier target for predators.
- If you need to walk at night, carry a flashlight and wear reflective clothing. Carry cab fare, bus fare or change for telephone calls in case you decide not to walk—and preferably, your cell phone. Keep some extra money separate from your wallet or purse for emergencies.
- Get a partner. Make arrangements to walk, run, bike, whatever, with others. The buddy system, there's safety in numbers.
- If you're out alone never, never, never hitchhike, and do not accept rides from anybody you do not know.
- Avoid distractions that will take you away from being fully aware of who and what is around you. When I use my iPod on a run or a hike, I leave one earpiece out. That way I can hear who's coming up behind me, and be aware of cars or other sounds—shouts, screams, stealthy footsteps— that will alert me to a potentially dangerous situation. If you're walking around town, be aware.
- Plan and use the safest and most direct route to your destination. Choose the busy, well-lighted streets and avoid isolated areas such as alleys, vacant lots, abandoned buildings and construction sites when walking and running. Avoid the shortcuts.

- Don't be an easy target. Use confident non-verbal signals so that you don't appear submissive. Observe people and activities around you. Look confident and purposeful when you walk.

- If you carry personal defensive tools such as pepper spray, Mace, those kind of things, understand legal and ethical requirements. Most importantly, seek a qualified trainer before carrying any personal defense tools.

- Keep your valuables out of sight. Money, credit cards, those kind of things. And if possible, avoid wearing expensive jewelry or carrying large amounts of cash. Keep your money and wallet inside your pockets of your jacket, jeans or purse. Do not carry your purse or handbag in your hand; secure it under your arm so it cannot be easily snatched.

- Walk or run near the curb, and use caution when walking or running near shrubbery, dark doorways and other places of concealment.

- Walk and run facing traffic so you can see approaching cars.

- Advise a loved one or a friend of the route you will be taking so they'll know where to look for you in case of an emergency. Let someone know where you'll be at all times.

- Tell your loved one when you expect to be back. You don't want to be stranded with an ankle sprain or break—or be recovering from an attack—any longer than is necessary for someone to realize something is wrong.

- Stay current with the events in your local area. Know what is going on in the local area so you can avoid walking, running or biking in areas that are criminally targeted.

- Be aware of adverse conditions: slippery areas, icy areas, steep hills, rocky areas and inclement weather.

- Take a dog if no one is available when you want to go out for a run or walk (a well-trained dog, not one you'll have to chase into traffic).

- Take your cell phone. Most running clothes have small pockets for keys and phones. Take it with you. Turn off the ringer if you want peace and quiet, but have it with you. It's a safety tool. Report any suspicious activity or persons to the police immediately.

- Get a medical check-up prior to getting involved in any outdoor activities.
- Don't overdo it. If you're out there running, biking, walking, hiking, whatever you're doing, and you've overdone it and you get sick or have some type of heart problem, or a medical emergency, now you can't defend yourself if you need to. Your personal safety is compromised because you've overdone it.
- Run, walk and bike during times when others are out, because you know there is safety in numbers.
- Have a plan. What would you do if you were confronted with an emergent or a threatening situation? What should you do? Consider taking CPR and first aid course.
- If you're followed or feel threatened by someone in a car, continually scream loudly, "STOP!" "FIRE!" and "NO!" Cross the street running in the opposite direction. If possible, obtain the license plate and description of the car and its occupants. And, of course, you're going to report that immediately to the police.
- If followed or threatened by someone who's walking, you want to continually use loud screams and yells and cross the street running the opposite direction. Go to a safe place with bright lights and people. Report it to the police immediately.
- Know the safe places on your route. If you need to get help right away, it's good to know safe zones such as certain stores that are safe, gas stations that stay open late at night, and the obvious places, police stations, fire departments, hospitals—those are all safe zones.

Also, When Biking...

- Keep your equipment in good repair. Keep your bike in good repair and carry the necessary tools in case of a breakdown. And, obviously, always wear your helmet when biking or rollerblading.
- Secure your bike when it's unattended. Use a high quality lock or cable. If using a rack, place the chain or cable through one wheel and the frame. You might want to secure both wheels if they have

quick releases. You don't want to come back to a one-wheeled bicycle.

- When biking, follow the rules of the road, use hand signals when turning, and ride defensively. I'm a triathlete, so I spend a lot of time on my road bike. But I ride in areas that are safer, that have low traffic, and I definitely prefer to ride on the bike paths.
- Equip your bike with reflectors and lights if biking during lower light hours.
- Above all, trust your instincts. If something doesn't seem right, it probably isn't.

Safety Committees at Work

OSHA, the Occupational Safety and Health Administration, mandates that all employers maintain a safe workplace for their employees. Many companies get their employees to help with this by having a Safety Committee. I was always interested in volunteering and being part of the safety committee where I worked, so that I could put forth my information and show my ideas and implement those ideas for a safer workplace. Those things are important to me, obviously. Consider getting involved in your company's safety committee. If you don't have a safety committee in your workplace, consider starting one.

Now that you've increased your awareness, you're probably noticing areas for improvement in your workplace. Submit your letters, ideas and e-mails to the safety committee for their consideration. Remember: your safety is *your* responsibility, even at work.

Know your co-workers. Who's around you? Who do you work with?

Make a commitment to look out for each other. If you have to leave your desk for a while, ask your co-worker to watch over your stuff. You never know the kind of troubles that might come into your workplace—an active shooter, a violent ex-boyfriend—so watch out for each other.

Post emergency numbers by every phone.

Report suspicious activities, individuals, packages or substances immediately to the police or security, depending on where you work. If that suspicious behavior is coming from a co-worker, pay particular attention.

There are always pre-incident indicators that a person is escalating, so let your supervisors know about your concerns so that appropriate personnel can intervene if they need to. Remember, people do NOT just snap. If your supervisor or the security personnel do not take you seriously, go to the police. Workplace violence can be prevented and mitigated through awareness and vigilance.

Notify maintenance immediately of any safety issues, such as broken door locks, broken windows, poor lighting, graffiti, etc.

Follow the safety guidelines for parking lots. Again, if possible, travel to and from work and parking areas with other people. Park in areas that are patrolled and well-lit after dark. Use security escorts during off hours and when others are not around.

Be safe in stairwells and elevators. Avoid using isolated, unused stairways in office buildings. If a suspicious-looking person follows you into an elevator, or someone makes you feel uncomfortable, step out of the elevator immediately. Get off as soon as possible. Trust your feelings. Often ladies don't want to do this because they're afraid they will be perceived as rude or even a bitch. You know what, ladies? So what? Who cares what other people think? Your safety is what you should think about, not someone else's feelings. Mr. Weirdo gets on the elevator with you, he gives you a weird feeling, just get right off. It doesn't matter what they think. It matters what you think! If you see a suspicious-looking person inside an elevator you're about to enter, don't get in. Wait for the next one. Again, who cares what they think? Trust your instincts.

When using elevators, stand near the control panel by the door so that you can easily press the alarm button in an emergency. In some locations, when that alarm is hit, it activates a camera in the elevator, so that the alerted security personnel can see what's going on in that elevator immediately.

Lock up your valuables, such as your purse, wallet, or keys, in desk drawers or other secured areas. Don't bring your valuables to work. Keep them at home. Don't advertise the amount of cash you are carrying.

Do not advertise your vacation plans at work, or times you will be away from home.

Be safe in restrooms. While at work, observe the security measures when using restrooms in your office buildings. If the facilities are locked, never leave the door unlocked or give the key to an unauthorized person. Do not enter the restroom if the lock appears broken or the door is ajar. If the facilities are not kept locked, enter cautiously and check the area thoroughly before closing the door behind you.

You probably don't think about that very often. You probably walk in the bathroom and head straight for the stall. But be careful, it's a private area which could pose a risk. Make it a habit to just kind of look around and be aware in that restroom environment.

In health care a number of years ago, medical centers implemented access-controlled restrooms for staff. So the staff have private, locked bathrooms now, with key-card access that the general public or patients can't use. Unfortunately, there was a significant number of incidents of staff being assaulted in restrooms.

Avoid working odd hours, or late hours, if at all possible. If you must work late or an odd shift, alert family members, friends or a security officer. If possible, have the security officer check on you from time to time. Ask a security officer, co-worker or an employee to escort you to your car or to public transportation. Do not walk to your car alone if you can avoid it at all.

Lock your doors when working evening hours and when leaving at night. If you work in an area that involves drugs or cash handling, use the appropriate safety and security precautions for cash handling and any type of pharmaceuticals or prescription drugs, if you're in that type of occupation.

Get more training. If you work in an at-risk area, such as an emergency department, school, behavioral health unit, prison, pharmacy, etc., get additional training on assaultive behavior—how to deescalate your clients or your patrons, how to defend against a physical attack. That's part of being prepared.

If you don't actively get involved in working with your employer to improve security in and around your workplace, it's going to be the same as it always has been. Now that you have read this book, you should have good insights into improving safety in your work place.

ENVIRONMENTAL SAFETY: BE SAFE WHEREVER YOU ARE

Traveling

When traveling to known and unknown destinations, you should definitely increase your environmental awareness. New environments mean new escape plans, new exit strategies, new people. Even if you've been there before, there are some precautions that you need to take, and it starts with keeping records.

Make copies of your passport, traveler's checks and credit card numbers to give to family members or a friend. Should you need to get copies of anything, you want those numbers and that information in a safe place so you can retrieve it when needed.

Be careful with your valuables. Carry your purse and your belongings close to your body. Keep your wallets in an inside pocket or coat pocket or front pocket. Safeguard your plane, bus, train, boat tickets and passport. Of course, never leave your luggage unattended, and report any unattended, suspicious baggage you find left alone.

Use all locking devices in your room. If you're in a hotel room, there are multiple locks. Use them.

Keep your valuables in a safe, whether it's in your room, or the hotel safe. Some hotels and motels also have safety deposit boxes. A lot of them have an electronic keypad that you set the lock yourself, so you program the number.

Always take your cash, credit cards and keys with you.

Never give your room number out to anybody.

Know the locations of the exits, elevators and phones in your hotel.

Leave the TV or radio on in your room when you leave. Make it appear that "you're home" so your room is less tempting to thieves.

Be especially alert in parking lots or garages. Call the front desk and ask if there's a security person on duty who can escort you during the evening hours.

Plan your routes carefully and use updated maps. When I went to Hawaii, my GPS didn't work. I didn't know that my GPS is only programmed for the 48 Continental states. Make sure you have accurate information.

Always travel on main roads. Shortcuts often get you in a predicament.

Always remove luggage and other valuables from your vehicle when stopping overnight. I travel in Southern California often in rental cars, or travel with a co-trainer who lives down there, and the old saying is, "leave them nothing." You leave nothing in the vehicle, nothing to tempt a thief to break the window and grab.

Airport and Luggage Safety

- Limit your carry-on baggage. You can only have one carry-on bag and one personal item. You don't want to take more than you can reasonably manage, anyway.
- Obviously, do not pack or bring prohibited items to the airport.
- You can legally carry up to four ounces of pepper spray, but you must put it in your checked baggage. (I travel with pepper spray frequently.)
- The little Kubatons that you can carry on your keychain also have to be checked. It's a pain, but it's important.
- Think carefully about the personal items you bring. Screeners may open your carry-on baggage and examine the contents, and checked bags are frequently opened and searched, too.
- Consider putting personal belongings in clear plastic bags to reduce the chance that a screener will have to handle them.
- Wait to wrap your gifts. If you're traveling during the holidays and bringing Christmas gifts, be aware that wrapped gifts may have to be opened for inspection. This applies to both carry-on and checked baggage.
- Control all bags and personal items. If they're out of sight, you don't know who might get to them or who might be handling them.
- Don't accept items at the airport or anytime when traveling. Don't accept any items to carry onboard a flight from anyone unknown to you.
- Report any unattended items in the airport or on an aircraft to the nearest airport police, airline or security personnel.
- Report suspicious behavior to the police or security immediately.

ENVIRONMENTAL SAFETY: BE SAFE WHEREVER YOU ARE

Overseas Travel

When traveling overseas, your awareness should really go up. If you're an American citizen, check the U.S. State Department's website prior to even booking any travel to certain countries; they update their website almost every day to alert us of risks and danger to Americans (www.state.gov). There are some countries that are simply not safe for Americans, based on terrorist attacks and just the overall threat.

Before Leaving Home:

- Make two photocopies of your passport identification page, airline tickets, driver's license and the credit cards that you plan to bring with you. Leave one photocopy with family member or friends at home; pack the other in a safe place, separate from where you carry your originals.
- Leave a copy of your itinerary with your family or friends at home in case they need to get in contact with you in the event of an emergency.
- Put your name, address and telephone numbers inside and outside of each piece of baggage. In overseas travel, you might want to identify some generic information on the outside of your bag so you can easily retrieve them at baggage claim areas.
- Make sure your affairs are in order before leaving home. Leave a current will, insurance documents and power of attorney with your family or close friend.
- Find out if your personal property insurance covers you for a loss or theft while abroad.
- Check on whether your health insurance covers you abroad. Some insurances don't. They're not going to cover you while overseas. If your health insurance will reimburse for medical care that you pay for abroad, normal health insurance does not pay for medical evacuation from a remote area or from a country where medical facilities are inadequate. Consider purchasing a short-term health and emergency assistance policy designed for travelers. Also make sure that the plan you purchase includes medical evacuation in the event of an accident or a serious illness.

- Discuss with your family what they would do in the event of an emergency.
- Book nonstop flights if possible. It reduces chances of complications—and reduces your luggage's exposure to unseen handlers. Avoid stopovers in high-risk airports.
- Learn a few phrases in the local language so you can signal for help. There are a lot of software programs out there that can help you learn those phrases quickly.
- Consider temporarily updating your phone for overseas coverage. With Verizon, when I go to Mexico I pay a little bit more to make calls back home. It's well worth it.

Packing/Traveling

- Minimize. Always try to travel light. You'll be more likely to have a free hand when you travel light. You'll also be less tired and less likely to set your luggage down, leaving it unattended.
- Try to minimize the time spent in public areas of an airport, which are less protected.
- Carry the minimum amount of valuables necessary for your trip and plan a place or places to conceal them. "Neck wallets" for passports, money, and ID, or concealed belt pouches can be tucked inside your shirt. Those are very popular for overseas travelers.
- Bring any medicines you need in your carry-on baggage. Keep medicines in their original labeled containers. If not, you might get in trouble based on what you have in that container. Bring copies of your prescriptions and the generic names for the drugs. If a medication is unusual or contains narcotics, carry a letter from your doctor verifying that you have a need to take this particular drug.
- Do not bring anything that you'd hate to lose. Just don't do it. Any special item that cannot be replaced, leave at home.
- Bring traveler's checks and one or two major credit cards instead of cash. Leave a copy of serial numbers of your traveler's checks with a friend or a relative at home. Carry your copy with you in a separate place, and as you cash the checks, cross them off the list

so you know which ones you've used and which ones you haven't. Countersign traveler's checks only in front of the person who will cash them. Change your traveler's checks only as you need them. Don't flash your cash around when paying a bill. Make sure your credit card is returned to you after every transaction. Only use authorized agents when exchanging money, buying airline tickets or souvenirs. Make a note of the credit limit on each credit card that you bring. In some countries, Americans have been arrested for innocently exceeding their credit limit.

- Pack an extra pair of glasses, if you wear them.
- Pack an extra set of passport photos along with the photocopy of your passport information page to make replacement of your passport easier in the event it is lost or stolen. There are also some online passport storage websites that you can research where you can store a copy of your passport online, so should you need to make a copy you can retrieve it via the internet.

Overseas Hotels

- Plan to stay at larger hotels. You'll most likely pay more, but they're going to have better security.
- Hotel safety experts recommend booking a room from the 2nd to the 7th floor above ground level; that deters easy entrance from outside, but is low enough for fire equipment to reach you.
- Keep your hotel door locked at all times.
- Meet visitors in the lobby.
- Do not leave money and other valuables in your hotel room while you are out; use the hotel safe.
- Read the safety instructions in your hotel room. It might be different than what you have here in the United States.
- Be sure to know where the nearest fire exits and alternate exits are located.
- Count the doors between your room and the nearest exit. That's an awareness of how long, how far it might take to get to that exit.

- Leave no personal or business papers in your hotel room. You never know who the maid is and what they might do with that information.

While on Vacation Overseas

- Register with U.S. embassy or consulate upon arrival.
- As much as possible, avoid luggage tags, clothing and behavior that may identify you as an American.
- Dress conservatively and do not wear expensive jewelry. You don't want to stick out. Don't make yourself a target. Avoid an appearance of being affluent.
- Keep a low profile and avoid loud conversations or arguments.
- Do not discuss travel plans or other personal matters with anyone, any strangers, anybody you do not know. Keep that to yourself.
- Only take taxicabs that are clearly identified with official markings. Be aware of unmarked cabs. Do not take a vehicle that is not clearly identified as a taxi. Be friendly, but be cautious about discussing personal matters or your itinerary or your plans, what you intend to do. Select your own taxicabs at random—sometimes, criminals will work in pairs, and a criminal will try to direct you to an accomplice's cab. Compare the face of the driver with the one posted on his license, which is usually posted somewhere in the cab. If possible, travel with others.
- Be cautious of pickpockets. Be aware of them, and know that they often have an accomplice who will jostle you, ask you for directions, or the time, or point to something spilled on clothing, or distract you by creating some other type of disturbance.
- Children and women can also be pickpockets. Beware of groups of vagrant children who create a distraction while picking your pocket.
- Wear the shoulder strap of your bag across your chest and walk with the bag away from the curb. Try to seem purposeful when you move about.
- Act as if you know where you're going and how you're going to get there.

- Know how to use a payphone and have the proper change or token on hand. The payphones overseas have some different codes.
- Avoid public demonstrations and other civil disturbances.
- Make note of emergency telephone numbers you may need.
- Do not use shortcuts, narrow alleys or poorly lit streets.
- Try not to travel alone or at night, period.
- Do not accept food or drink from strangers. Criminals have been known to drug food or drink offered to passengers. Criminals may also spray sleeping gas into train compartments.
- Watch for people following you or loiterers observing your comings and goings. Be aware of the people who are aware of what you are doing.
- Keep a mental note of safe havens such as police stations or hospitals.
- Let someone you trust know what your travel plans are, and keep them informed if you change your plans.
- Avoid predictable times and routes of travel and report any suspicious activity to the local police and the nearest U.S. embassy or consulate.
- Formulate a plan of action for a bomb explosion or nearby gunfire. Those things can happen overseas as well as here in the U.S.
- If your possessions are lost or stolen, report the loss immediately to the local police. Keep a copy of the police report for insurance claims and as an explanation of your plight.

Rental Cars

- When you rent a car, choose a type that is commonly available for that location.
- Ask that markings identifying it as a rental car be removed.
- Choose a car with universal locks and power windows.
- An air conditioner allows you to drive with the windows closed, which you'll want to do. Keep the car doors locked at all times.
- Wear seatbelts.
- As much as possible, avoid driving at night.

- Do not leave your valuables in the car.
- Do not park your car on the street overnight.
- Never pick up hitchhikers anywhere, especially abroad.
- Do not get out of the car if there are suspicious-looking individuals nearby. Drive away.
- Carjackers and thieves operate at gas stations, parking lots and city traffic and along the highway. Be suspicious of anyone who hails you or tries to get your attention when you are in or near your car. And again, drive with your car windows closed in crowded streets or anywhere.
- Criminals use ingenious ploys. They may pose as Good Samaritans, offering help for tires that are flat or that they have made flat. They may flag down a motorist, asking for assistance then steal your luggage or your car. Usually they work in groups, one person carrying on the pretense while the others rob you.
- Other criminals get your attention with abuse, either trying to drive you off the road or causing an accident by rear ending you or creating a fender bender. Follow the same vehicle precautions abroad that you would at home. In some urban areas, thieves do not waste time on ploys. They simply smash car windows at traffic lights, grab your valuables or your car and get away.

The laws are different in other countries, so you want to know the law because you're going to be subject to its jurisdiction. When you're in a foreign country and you're subject to its laws and its jurisdiction, not the protection of the U.S. Constitution, you can be arrested for actions that may be legal or considered minor infractions at home. U.S. citizens have been arrested abroad for drug violations, possession of firearms, photography, and purchasing antiques.

The first and best protection from terrorism is to avoid traveling to unsafe areas where there has been a persistent record of terrorist attacks or kidnappings. Avoid obvious targets such as places where Americans and Westerners are known to congregate.

My intent with all these guidelines and rules is not to scare you. Remember, hyper-vigilance is counter-productive. But following basic, common sense guidelines will keep you safe. Read, and re-read this chapter. Make a commitment to adopt one new habit a month to keep you safe. Once that safety practice is habitual, pick up another one. Your safety is first and foremost your responsibility.

"The notion of freedom proclaimed by the modern world is anti-discipline. But true freedom cannot be separated from discipline."

— Matthew Kelly

Chapter 10

Self-Discipline

I wasn't born a personal safety expert. I had to learn all these things, too, and I am constantly working on improving my AVADE® skills: my awareness, my vigilance, and my avoidance. I am always looking for better ways to teach people how to defend themselves. I am always thinking about new or better escape plans or routes.

But I still have to discipline myself, too. You remember that Kubotan, the mini-baton on my keychain? Since I can't carry it on airplanes, I used to take it off my keys and leave it in my vehicle, parked at the airport while I was traveling. But I didn't always remember to put it back on my keychain when I got back from my trip. Not exactly vigilant, right?

I have a friend who always, ALWAYS, wears a Leatherman utility knife on his belt (he is trained in martial arts, and is skilled enough to use it as a weapon, but mostly he carries it because it's very useful). He can't take it on a plane, obviously, so when he gets to the airport, just before he hands over his suitcase, he takes his utility knife off his belt and puts it in an easy-to-access pocket of his checked bag. The first thing he does when he reclaims his bag is put that utility knife back on his belt.

I made a commitment to do that, too. Now, my Kubotan goes in my checked suitcase, and I always have it with me when I'm out of town. I wasn't very disciplined about that personal safety tool, but now I am.

So What Are You Going to Do About It?

Now you have all the information you need to stay safe. Now you know that your incredibly powerful mind is your best asset in keeping you safe. So what are you going to do with this information? If you do nothing with your new-found knowledge, it's just like watching TV. It's just information. By itself, it doesn't create change in your life. You have to decide to do something about it. You have to take responsibility, and discipline yourself to create new, safer habits and practices. You have to commit.

If you want change in any area of your life, you must choose to learn, and grow, and get out of your comfort zone. That's what this chapter is about: committing to growing in the realm of your personal safety.

In the thirty years I've been a student of personal safety—fifteen of which, I've also been a teacher—I have developed ten steps that will get you to that goal, to that place where personal safety is second nature for you. But just like any coach, I can't do your push-ups for you. I can't park your car and lock it for you. I can't drink water for you. I can't do the things that you know you need to do. It's all about you. It's all about that personal responsibility, that personal self-discipline with your safety and your life. So here are the ten steps for personal safety self-discipline.

1. Train

Lots of people talk about training, but very few actually follow through. Physical training can be demanding, time-consuming, and, to some people, boring. But when we're talking about training for personal safety, it starts with the mind.

Write those mental movies. Do it right now. I practice all of my tactics and techniques in my mind's eye, and the beautiful part about that is that, my technique is always perfect. I always win. I'm always successful. But it takes focus to do that, to see myself going through the scenario, the situation.

What's your biggest fear around your safety? Think about it, and write the mental movie where you come out safe. My friend told me her biggest fear was being attacked in a parking lot while buckling her two young children into their car seats. That's when her awareness is on her children, and someone could come up behind her without her knowing it. So I told her to write that mental movie: she's scanning the area to make sure it's safe, ducking down into her car and getting her kids buckled as quickly as possible. Visualizing what self-defense tactics she would use if grabbed from behind. Thinking about, and mentally practicing screaming "Stop! FIRE! NO!" She told me that practicing that in her mind made her much faster getting her kids in their seats—and that's just safer all around. She's exposed for less time, her car doors are open for less time—and it's nice that she's standing outside the car in cold or rain or snow for less time!

I want to be clear that I am not discounting physical training. I was a professional fighter, I'm a black belt in Karate, and a triathlete. Obviously, I think physical training is very important. But there's a balance.

Michael Jordan was the best basketball player of all time. His teammates said he was the first one on, and the last one off, the practice court every day. But Michael Jordan knows how important mental preparation is, too: before every game, he'd sit in the locker room and run through the game in his mind, seeing himself scoring, seeing himself winning. And he did win—over and over, for years and years as a college player, a professional, and an Olympian.

As we get older, we stop consciously daydreaming. It's probably because we're discouraged from it growing up: "Get your head out of the clouds!" "Get focused!" "Get with the program!" But it's really important to allow ourselves to consciously daydream and create these visions and images in our mind of what we want and how we want to live.

The physical part of training is vital, though, no question. You've learned all about avoiding danger and escape plans, but if your body is not physically ready to move, you're going to have a problem. It's up to you to do some exercise, to be in reasonable shape to be able to run from a situation; adrenaline can only do so much. And that's aside from the ability to use any self-defense training you've had—being able to use your hand, your foot, or your knee to defend yourself against a physical attack.

It doesn't take three or four hours every night. I'm not talking about months or years of martial arts training. A few times a week, twenty or thirty minutes a session, that's it. As for self-defense techniques, practice them. If you don't have a partner, at least practice your part, with visualization. Practice how you would break a bear hold, or kick at a knee from the floor. Train your body and your mind so you can respond when you need to.

2. Set Goals

Goal setting got really popular in the 1980s. It became kind of a buzz phrase: "goal setting" meant you were focused, you were driven, you were serious. I think a lot of people jumped on that bandwagon, but never followed through. So now you bring up "setting goals" and people roll their eyes; it brings back a memory of that flaky brother-in-law who was always spouting off about his goals… and never actually accomplishing anything.

But successful people set goals and accomplish great things. Setting goals is committing to something higher than yourself. Goals—with disciplined action—become habits. Everything else is just a wish, a fantasy or a dream.

I set goals all the time. Almost every week, things I want to accomplish—how many miles I'll run, how many new clients I'll contact, remembering to put my Kubotan back on my keychain!

What are your personal safety goals? Take a minute right now. Write them down—there's something magical that happens when you put it on paper. It makes it real. Whether it's increasing your awareness, being more vigilant, whatever, write some things out.

Be specific: "I will lock my door behind me as soon as I walk in the house," "I will have my keys ready to unlock my car before I walk out the door," "When I'm running [walking/hiking], I will keep one ear phone out, so I can hear what's going on around me." Write down ten goals right now. Then, spend three weeks concentrating on each one. (Experts say that it takes twenty-one days for an action to become a habit.) In less than year, you'll have ten new personal safety habits. Of course, in addition to those habits, you're also training yourself to be more aware, and you've learned to be more vigilant, and avoid dangerous situations.

You've got to set the goal. If not, you're just dreaming about it. It's just a wish. It's something you should do, but you never do. Commit right now. Write it down, and focus on it for twenty-one days in a row.

3. Strive for Balance

You need balance in your life. To be mentally, physically, and spiritually healthy, to create harmony in your life, you need balance.

I constantly evaluate myself. For instance, am I stimulating myself enough mentally? Am I reading enough books? Am I engaging in thoughtful communication enough with people? Am I pushing myself to engage in eustress (positive stress for certain projects)? My editor was recently telling me that she was so happy about the work she was doing for me on this book, because it engaged her mental focus, and she got to use that part of her brain and her talents that give her real satisfaction. That's the kind of mental balance that we need in our life.

Balance with your body and physical health is not only physical training it's also your physical presence—are you aware of what your body can and can't do? What messages are you sending with your body? Do you appear confident, or meek and timid? That's physical balance, including your overall health.

Remember "synchronicity"? That experience of feeling connected to other people is part of the intuitive side of us. (The example we used was thinking about someone you hadn't talked to in a long time, and then they email or call out of the blue.) When you feel in balance, things flow and you feel more connected. You feel more at peace and in harmony in your overall life. In that place of clarity, you hear the voice of intuition more clearly, and you trust it more—and that keeps you safe. It directs you away from dangerous people or dangerous situations. Remember the mother who raged at the man who walked away with her son? She trusted her intuition that he wasn't safe—and she was right. He was a pedophile. She trusted her intuition above everything else—above social mores, worrying about hurting someone's feelings—and she kept her son safe.

You need balance in your environments, too. Your environments can push you forward, be positive and uplifting, but they can also bring you down. And I don't mean only physical environments—your house, your car, your workplace—I mean your relationship environments, too. Spend your time with people who fill you up, not people who drain you. It's hard to be aware, and vigilant and use all your personal safety skills when you're emotionally and mentally exhausted from draining partners, friends, relatives, or co-workers.

Find that balance: mind, body, spirit and environment. It will help you live in harmony, live in peace, and live with positive purpose, and grow as a person. That balance will help you be aware and vigilant, it will keep you connected to your intuition, and it will help keep you safe.

4. PAVE Your Way to Personal Safety

I wear two bracelets, one on each wrist. They say: "Higher Awareness" and "PAVE". PAVE is an acronym I came up with just a few years ago to describe this part of the spiritual, personal safety that I personally aspire to, and to live in on a daily basis. The acronym means:

Pray
Affirm
Visualize
Empower

Prayer: My wife, Genelle Fowler, is a prayer warrior. She spends a tremendous amount of time praying to God. Genelle describes prayer as an act of reaching out to the God almighty in submission to His power and grace. She prays for everything: Me, our five kids and one grandchild, our business, our finances, friends and family, our safety and protection, and everything else that life hands us. She has been instrumental in encouraging me to pray. So now I, like her, pray for everything in our life, too. I would encourage you, the reader, to pray to God almighty for your safety and anything and everything else going on in your life right now.

Prayer is a foundation. It helps you to focus on God and ask Him to keep you safe. I have found that to be incredibly powerful in keeping myself and my family safe: I am focused on staying safe, I put that out there, I am connected to God and my intuition, and I probably avoid so many possible dangers in a day or a week, I don't even realize it.

Affirmation: Psychologists tell us that we have approximately 40,000 to 50,000 thoughts per day. That amazes me. Have you ever asked yourself, "What am I thinking right now?" or "What was I thinking?" You can probably say what you're thinking about: right now, you're thinking about this book. But are your thoughts positive and affirming? Or are they negative? Remember learning about kinesiology and muscle testing? Positive thoughts make you strong; negative thoughts literally weaken your muscles. So, are you safer when you're physically strong, or weak?

Be conscious of what you're thinking. Think affirming, positive thoughts. Affirm with statements or declarations about what you really want in your life. I repeat an affirmation almost daily of what I want in my life, and it goes like this:

"I am healthy, I am wealthy, I am strong, I am young, I am powerful, I am loving, I am harmonious, and I am successful."

It's not a mantra or a chant that doesn't mean anything. I have energy when I say this affirmation. In fact, when I first started doing this a number of years ago, I would actually look into the mirror and repeat the affirmation. It would really lift me up. At first I didn't believe everything I said, but now I truly believe it—you know the old saying, "Fake it 'til you make it." I affirm to myself that I am healthy, safe, strong, etc.—all the positive things that I want to affirm in my mind and declare to the universe. When I am declaring that over and over, affirming it to myself, I guarantee you I have a confident presence that deters predators. I am not an easy target.

Visualize: Now you know all about mental movies and how important that mental training is. Visualize yourself winning or surviving any altercation. Visualize yourself staying safe and being happy. Again, those positive thoughts and beliefs will literally make you stronger.

You can visualize for everything you want in your life. Can you visualize that new car you want? Can you visualize your dream home? Can you visualize that perfect relationship? It all starts in the mind's eye. W. Clement Stone, an incredibly successful entrepreneur and mentor to thousands of people said, "Whatever the mind can conceive it can achieve."

What are you seeing? What are you visualizing? What are you creating? A life where you're safe and protected, or a life where you're constantly under attack or threat from predators? Visualize using your awareness and vigilance to help you avoid anything dangerous. Hopefully, you'll never even need to worry about self-defense or escape.

Empower. You've empowered yourself by reading this book. You have tactics, techniques and the right mindset now to keep yourself safe. Now empower others. Share these principles with them. Teach them what you've learned. Pay it forward!

I live by the Godly principle, "give and you shall receive." I try to do that every day, to be thoughtful, to give praise and appreciation to as many people as I can. I empower people to keep doing the good they're doing, and I feel empowered that I gave someone some validation that their efforts are appreciated.

PAVE your way every day. Pray, affirm, visualize and empower. It's the spirit filled side of personal safety.

5. Meditate

When I was a kid, my mom would get up early for work almost every day, and she'd sit at the kitchen table with her cup of coffee. She wouldn't read anything, she would just sit there and prepare herself for her day. I remember asking her, "Why do you do that? What are you doing, Mom? Why do you just sit there quietly? The TV's not on, the radio's not on, you don't have a paper or anything. What's that all about?" And she said, "David, this is my 'veg' time." What she called "vegging out" is what other people call meditation—just being quiet and allowing her mind and her body to get prepared for the day's events.

There are literally dozens—if not hundreds—of ways to meditate. There are hundreds of books and CDs that can teach you how. I don't think it really matters how you meditate, but that quieting of the mind helps clear away the mental clutter. That clarity helps you be present in your day, which, you know now, is one of the keys to keeping yourself safe. Samurai warriors spent as much time in meditation—preparing their minds and bodies—as they did physically training.

However you do it, just work on quieting your mind. I just encourage that you try it. I like to meditate while I'm running; other people have to be lying down, eyes closed. You don't have to do it for hours a day. At first, just sit quietly for a minute and focus on your breath. It's a great way to get started. Do it every day. Start to add time, make it a little longer.

Many teachers talk about meditation as a supplement to living a balanced life. For some practiced people, fifteen minutes in meditation is like a four hour nap. I find that intriguing—through calming the mind and body, we create vitality and we prepare ourselves for life, for the events that will come.

6. Believe You Can

People get all upset when I tell them that they're full of BS. But we all are. We're all full of Belief Systems, for better or for worse. They're ingrained. When you really think about, when you really go deep within yourself, you may find surprising things that you believe about money, politics, or religion. You also might find some surprising beliefs about your own safety. Ask yourself, what do you believe about your safety? Do you believe that you have the right to be safe? Do you believe that you're capable of defending yourself, should something happen? Do you believe that others will come to your rescue? Do you believe that there's a higher source that also is part of your safety? Now, if you believe you can't do anything about certain situations, guess what? You can't. Henry Ford said it best:

"Whether you believe that you can or you can't, you are right."

Think about what you believe when it comes to safety, when it comes to protecting yourself, when it comes to aggression, violence and crime. If you find beliefs that don't serve you, that won't help keep you safe, change those beliefs. After I got beaten up when I was twelve years old, I *wanted* to believe that I could take care of myself, that I could defend myself. So I went out and made that a reality.

What do you believe about that? Do you believe that you can live a safe, harmonious, and productive life? I know I do, and I encourage you to believe the same way. Your belief systems will manifest in your body and in your mind, and become a reality. I'm proof of that. That skinny little twelve-year-old victim became a black belt and Karate champion within a few years, because I believed I could.

What do you believe?

7. Read to Succeed

For my work, in addition to studying personal safety, and criminal behavior, and the psychology of predators, I have studied the psychology of success. In all my study of successful people, I have realized one important thing: successful people read. Successful people are constantly increasing their knowledge base.

In the bibliography and reference guide at the end of this book you'll see a list of recommendations for books that I've read, and that I encourage you to read. They're books that will add to what you've learned here, and will enhance your ability to be safe. They're books you can recommend to your friends and your loved ones.

I decided to write this book a couple of years ago. But I kept procrastinating because I thought I needed to learn more. I finally wrote the first manuscript for this book about two years ago, and then it just sat on the shelf. But I finally realized, I have enough knowledge to impart to make a complete book. I will continue to read. I'll to continue to study and learn, and as I accumulate more knowledge and synthesize it into information that contributes to personal safety, I'll share that, too. I will always read and study and learn, because there is always something new out there, some new way to approach and understand personal safety.

8. Formulate Your Personal Mission Statement

When I first read *Seven Habits of Highly Effective People,* by Stephen Covey, something that jumped out at me was the process of writing out a mission statement. I developed my own mission statement, and over the years it's changed and it's grown and it's developed into a description of the person I aspire to be.

In my company's Security Oriented Customer Service (SOCS™) training program (www.SOCStraining.com), I teach security personnel how to provide the best service they can. Part of it is the choice of mission. We've all heard about organizational mission statements; almost every major organization in our country has a mission statement. Some of those organizations have departmental mission statements, but the concept of a personal mission statement is often skimmed over. In the SOCS™ training, we ask security personnel to commit to creating a personal mission statement, and it's huge for them.

Our feedback from that one piece of the training is just amazing. People tell us things like, "It really made me think about my values, my belief system and really where I was going in life." Does that help us line up with our organizational or departmental mission statements? It usually does. When you're a better person, it's not compartmentalized; you're not only going to be better at home, you're going to be better at work, in your relationships, etc. When you're a better person, you're more valuable to your department and your organization.

Your mission statement illustrates the end of the path that you're on. It describes the person you intend to be, who you aspire to be. My mission statement is:

> I am so happy and grateful that I am healthy, strong, young and powerful, doing all the mental, physical and spiritual activities that I choose. The success I experience daily by teaching, writing and learning is truly amazing, and I am blessed. I am on purpose and feel harmony and love in my life by sharing my life with others through thoughtful communication and understanding. Daily, I pray, affirm, visualize and empower to achieve the most success, happiness and harmony in my life and in others.

That's my mission statement. It took me a while to come up with it. It has also changed and developed as I grew—and I'm still growing, so it could change again. But it's the path that I want to take. It's the person I want to be.

That's what a mission statement really is about. It's your compass. It's your lighthouse. When it gets dark, or foggy, you have stress in your life, it keeps you focused on what direction you are going.

How does this relate to personal safety? Well, when you know what direction you are going, it's easier to stay on the path. You will inherently *avoid* things that don't mesh with your mission statement. And your mission statement will be about happiness and fulfillment, right? Not sending you down dark alleys where predators lurk.

I've seen what a huge impact this exercise has on people, so I want to encourage you to think about a mission statement, and write it out. Start with this: What are your values? Write out some values and plug them into a mission statement. It's going to take time to develop that and really uncover where you want to go, and who you want to be. But when you do, your compass will be set. You will more easily stay on the path to be the person who you want to be.

9. Be Authentic

When you are authentic, it is the real you, not someone else's version of who you should be or how they think you should act. So if you commit to creating a mission statement, and living it, you are living in authenticity. You are being your authentic self. Nobody else writes that mission statement, nobody else decides what path you're going to follow, who you want to be, what you aspire to be. That's all on you. That's what being authentic is about.

Being authentic is also about finding that goodness inside you. I personally call this goodness inside of us, the Jesus or God that is within us. Really living that inspires others. It helps them to be authentic as well. You probably know someone who embodies this. Someone who has deep-seated values and convictions, who knows who they are, and who is full of joy, love and peace. When you spend time with those people, you feel filled up, and joyous, and energized.

Be the authentic you. Realize that that spiritual side of you is important and through discipline, commitment, determination and understanding, you will be that authentic person and live the life that is destined for you.

When you live this way, you emanate confidence and peace and joy. And those things are literally predator repellent!

10. Inspire Others

My goal in all the training I do, all the work I do, and in writing this book was to inspire you. I want to inspire you to live in joy, not fear. I want to lift you up, so you learn to use AVADE® skills to feel safe. I want to empower you with knowledge, and inspire you to get in better shape, to be more aware, to create personal safety habits. That inspires me.

What can you do in your personal life to inspire others? What can you do to inspire others to lead a safer life? Maybe it's in your actions, your words, your thoughts and your feelings. So how are you living your life today? Are you positive or are you negative? Ask yourself, Am I looking for the best in all? Am I looking at the cup half full or am I looking at it half empty? Having that positive optimistic attitude versus a pessimistic attitude is inspiring. When you adopt all the personal safety habits and practices that you've learned in this book, and you show others that habitually being safety-conscious does not mean being paranoid, does not mean seeing a predator behind every bush, rather that it's a higher form of awareness that is actually liberating. Do this and you will inspire others to think about their personal safety more.

When you saw this chapter's title, did you deflate a little? Did you think, "Oh man, this is the part that's homework! Now I have to discipline myself!" If you did think that at the beginning, I hope you see that discipline doesn't confine you or limit you. Self-discipline sets you free to be the best person you can be.

Conclusion

M y hope, my wish, my prayer for you is that you'll follow through with AVADE®. That you'll take this information, you'll commit to using it in your own life, and you'll stand as a model to others of how to live safely, without fear.

Now that I've taught you what I know, I hope you will do the same. Pay it forward. Share it with another person.

It seems kind of backwards; you might be thinking, "I just learned this, and you want me to go out and teach it to my friend, my family, my coworkers?" But as I share it with you, I become more familiar with it. Every time I teach a class, people ask me questions that help me think about these things differently. When you share it with another person, you learn the information in a whole new way, you'll dive deeper into it, understand it better, know it on another level, believe it, and actually use it.

Whatever has really resonated with you in this book—whether it's awareness, vigilance, avoidance, interpersonal communication skills, understanding time and distance, having escape strategies for all environments, knowing personal safety environmental factors, knowing how to deal with your stress—whatever it is that hit you, I encourage you to follow through, to be disciplined, to take the action and to use it in your life. That's why I wrote this book—so you could be safer in your life and in every environment and in everything that you do.

Take a look at the reference material and decide to read some additional books, or to reread this book, which really helps. Humans learn through repetition. You read it once, and then you read it again and there are going to be some things that jump out at you and hit you in a different way.

These final words are not the end, they're a starting point. I sincerely and passionately hope that the material presented here in this book is a change for you, is motivation for you to seek out safer ways to live, and in doing so you become an authentic person. Change your belief system to a higher level. Get out of that victim mentality. Recognize that there might be more to life than you thought. That you can deal with fear, that you can deal with stress in life, and that you can move forward, instead of stagnating.

I really hope that you make the commitment, that you take the challenge and you incorporate what you've learned into your life. Every journey begins with the first initial step. You took that first step by reading this book. One person at a time can make a difference, and I know you can make a difference not only in your life but the lives of others. That's my hope for this book: to make that difference with one person, and for that person to teach other people and other people and other people, for it to be exponential.

Be Safe and God Bless You!

Bibliography and Reference Guide

Publications

Adams, Terry. *Seminar Production Business: Your Step-by-Step Guide to Success*. Canada: Entrepreneur Press, 2003.

Andersen, Peter A. *The Complete Idiot's Guide to Body Language*. Indianapolis, IN: Alpha Books, 2004.

Andrews, Andy. *The Traveler's Gift: Seven Decisions that Determine Personal Success*. Nashville, TN: Nelsen Books, 2002.

Arapakis, Maria. *Soft Power: How to Speak Up, Set Limits, and Say No Without Losing Your Lover, Your Job, or Your Friends*. New York: Warner Books, Inc., 1990.

Artwhohl, Alexis and Loren Christensen. *Deadly Force Encounters: What Cops Need to Know to Mentally and Physically Prepare for and Survive a Gunfight*. Boulder, CO: Paladin Press, 1997.

Booth, Nate, Dr. *The Diamond Touch: How to Get What You Want by Giving People What They Uniquely Desire*. Encinitas, CA: Harrison Acorn Press, 1998.

Byrnes, John D. *Before Conflict: Preventing Aggressive Behavior*. Lanham, MD: Scarecrow Press, 2002.

Canfield, Jack and Janet Switzer. *The Success Principles: How to Get from Where You Are to Where You Want to Be*. New York: Harper Collins Publishers, 2005.

Carlaw, Peggy and Vasudha Kathleen Deming. *The Big Book of Customer Service Training Games: Quick, Fun Activities for All Customer Facing Employees*. New York: McGraw-Hill, 1999.

Carnegie, Dale. *How to Win Friends & Influence People*. New York: Pocket Books, 1936.

Chodron, Thubten. *Working with Anger*. Ithaca, NY: Snow Lion Publication, 2001.

Covey, Stephen R. *The 7 Habits of Highly Effective People: Powerful Lessons in Personal Change*. New York: Fireside, 1989.

Day, Laura. *Practical Intuition*. New York: Villard Books, 1996.

DeBecker, Gavin. *The Gift of Fear*. New York: Dell Publishing, 1997.

Dimitrius, Jo-Ellen and Wendy Patrick Mazzarella. *Reading People: How to Understand People and Predict Their Behavior—Anytime, Anyplace*. New York: Ballantine Books, 1999.

Eckman, Paul. *Emotions Revealed, Second Edition: Recognizing Faces and Feelings to Improve Communication and Emotional Life*. New York: Henry Holt & Company, 2007.

Eckman, Paul. *Telling Lie: Clues to Deceit in the Marketplace, Politics and Marriage*. New York: W.W. Norton & Company, 1991.

Gallo, Carmine. "Inspire Your Audience: 7 Keys to Influential Presentations." Published paper, December 31, 2008.

Gawain, Shakti. *Creative Visualization: Use the Power of Your Imagination to Create What You Want in Your Life*. Novato, CA: New World Library, 2002.

BIBLIOGRAPHY AND REFERENCE GUIDE

Gawain, Shakti. *Developing Intuition: Practical Guidance for Daily Life*. Novato, CA: New World Library, 2000.

Gladwell, Malcolm. *Blink: The Power of Thinking Without Thinking*. New York: Little, Brown & Company, 2005.

Goleman, Daniel. *Emotional Intelligence: 10th Anniversary Edition; Why It Can Matter More Than IQ*. New York: Bantam Books, 2006.

Gray, John. *Men Are from Mars, Women Are from Venus*. New York: Harper Collins Publishers, 1992.

Grossman, Dave and Loren W. Christensen. *On Combat: The Psychology and Physiology of Deadly Conflict in War and in Peace*. Illinois: PPCT Research, 2004.

Harrell, Keith. *Attitude is Everything: 10 Life-Changing Steps to Turning Attitude Into Action*. New York: Harper Collins Publishing, 1999.

Hawkins, David R., M.D., Ph.D. *Power vs. Force: The Hidden Determinants of Human Behavior*. Carlsbad, CA: Hay House, Inc., 1995.

Jung, Carl. "Synchronicity: An Acausal Connecting Principle." 1952.

Kane, Lawrence A. and Loren W. Christensen. *Surviving Armed Assaults: A Martial Artist's Guide to Weapons, Street Violence and Countervailing Force*. Boston: YMAA Publication Center, 2006.

Mackay, Harvey. *Harvey Mackay's Column This Week*. Weekly e-mail publication, www.harveymackay.com.

Maggio, Rosalie. *How to Say It: Choice Words, Phrases, Sentences, and Paragraphs for Every Situation*. New York: Prentice Hall Press, 2001.

Maltz, Maxwell, M.D. *Psycho-Cybernetics: A New Way to Get More Living Out Of Life*. New York: Essandress, 1960.

Marcinko, Richard. *The Rogue Warrior's Strategy for Success*. New York: Pocket Books, 1997.

Medina, John. *Brain Rules: 12 Principles for Surviving and Thriving at Work, Home, and School*. Seattle: Pear Press, 2008.

Mehrabian, Albert. *Silent Messages: Implicit Communication of Emotions and Attitudes, Second Edition*. Belmont, California: Wadsworth, 1981.

Morgenstern, Julie. *Never Check E-Mail In the Morning: And Other Un expected Strategies for Making Your Work Life Work*. New York: Simon & Schuster, 2005.

Murphy, Joseph, Dr. *The Power of Your Subconscious Mind*. New York: Bantam Books, 2000.

Musashi, Miyamoto and Thomas Cleary. *The Book of Five Rings*. Boston: 2003. Shambala, Boston & London 2003.

Ouellette, Roland W. *Management of Aggressive Behavior*. Powers Lake, WI: Performance Dimension Publishing, 1993.

Parker, S.L. *212° The Extra Degree™*. www.walkthetalk.com: The Walk the Talk Co., 2005.

Peale, Norman Vincent. *Six Attitudes for Winners*. Wheaton, IL: Tyndale House Publishers, Inc., 1989.

Peale, Norman Vincent. *The Power of Positive Thinking*. New York: Ballantine Books, 1956.

Pease, Allan and Barbara. *The Definitive Book of Body Language*. New York: Bantam Dell, 2004.

Rail, Robert R. *The Unspoken Dialogue: Understanding Body Language and Controlling Interviews and Negotiations*. Kansas City, KS: Varro Press, 2001.

BIBLIOGRAPHY AND REFERENCE GUIDE

Ratey, John J. *Spark: The Revolutionary New Science of Exercise and the Brain*. New York: Little, Brown and Co., 2008.

Satir, Virginia, John Banmen, Jane Gerber, and Maria Gomori. *Satir Model: Family Therapy and Beyond*. Palo Alto, CA: Science and Behavior Books, 1991.

Thompson, George. *Verbal Judo: The Gentle Art of Persuasion*. New York: Quill William Morrow, 1993.

Turner, James T. *Violence in the Medical Care Setting*. Rockville, MD: Aspen Systems Corporation, 1984.

Tzu, Sun. *The Art of War, Samuel Griffith Interpretation*. London: Oxford University Press, 1993.

Bottom Line Publications Editors. *The World's Greatest Treasury of Health Secrets*. Stamford, CT: 2006.

Harvard Business School Press. *The Results Driven Manager: Dealing with Difficult People*. Boston: 2005.

Webster's Dictionary. New York: Modern Promotions/Publishers, 1984.

DVDs, CDs, and Downloads

Chart House Learning. *"Fish" Catch the Energy—Release the Potential*. DVD. fishphilosophy.com

Carnegie, Dale. *Golden Book*. www.dalecarnegie.com

Covey, Stephen R. *The 8th Habit: From Effectiveness to Greatness*. Better Life Media, DVD and CD, 2004.

Gray, John. *Beyond Mars and Venus*. Better Life Media, DVD and CD, 2004.

Media Partners. "I'll Be Back" Customer Service with Bob Farrell, DVD.

Sjodin, Terri L. *New Sales Speak: The 9 Biggest Sales Presentation Mistakes and How to Avoid Them.* Better Life Media, DVD and CD 2004.

Tracy, Brian. *Secrets of Self-Made Millionaires: Learnable Skills and Qualities That Can Turn You Into a Millionaire.* Better Life Media, DVD and CD, 2005.

Seminars

Canfield, Jack and Jim Bunch. *The Ultimate Life Workshop: 7 Strategies for Creating the Ultimate Life.* Live Workshop, February 2008.

Website References

Personal Safety Training, Inc.:
www.AVADEtraining.com
www.personalsafetytraining.com
www.socstraining.com
www.wpvprevention.com
www.tribalsecuritytraining.com

Other References:

www2.massgeneral.org/police/police_directory.htm
www.biologyreference.com/Po-Re/Predation-and-Defense.html
www.crimedoctor.com
www.dictionary.reference.com
www.easy-strategy.com/strategy-definition.html
www.dps.mo.gov/HomelandSecurity/documents/Active%20Shooter/DHS%20ActiveShooter_Response%20Booklet.pdf
www.hms.harvard.edu/ombuds/techniques/index.html
http://en.wikipedia.org/wiki/Awareness
http://en.wikipedia.org/wiki/Fight-or-flight_response
http://en.wikipedia.org/wiki/Fixing_Broken_Windows
http://evolwithin.wordpress.com/2008/01/23/fight-flight-freeze/
http://definitions.uslegal.com/s/self-defense/

BIBLIOGRAPHY AND REFERENCE GUIDE

http://dictionary.bnet.com/definition/Interpersonal+Communication.html

http://necsi.org/projects/evolution/co-evolution/pred-prey/co-evolution_
predator.html

www.knowledgebank.irri.org/IPM/biocontrol/Characteristics_of_a_
predator.htm

www.lapdonline.org/prevent_crime

www.lectlaw.com/def/d030.htm

www.legal-explanations.com/definitions/self-defense.htm

www.ncvc.org

www.securityinfowatch.com

www.selfgrowth.com/articles/the_myth_of_vigilance.html

www.strategicconcepts-ca.com

www.thefreedictionary.com/predator

www.webmd.com/balance/stress-management/tc/guided-imagery-topic-
overview

www.wikipedia.org

www.workplaveviolence911.com

"The only way to deal with conflict and avoid violence of any type is through awareness, knowledge and defensive training."

— David Fowler, President of PSTI

Training Courses for YOU and YOUR Agency

D avid Fowler, President of PSTI, specializes in nationally recognized training programs that empower individuals, increase confidence and promote proactive preventative solutions.

PSTI Offers You:

• On-Site Training
• Instructor Seminars
• Train-the-Trainer
• Combo Classes
• Scenario Training
• Books and CDs
• Videos and DVDs

Call today!

Toll Free (866) 773-7763 outside the US (208) 664-5551
Find Us on the Web!
www.PersonalSafetyTraining.com
www.AVADEtraining.com
www.SOCStraining.com

OSHA, Labor & Industries, Joint Commission, State Healthcare Laws, and the Department of Health all recognize that programs like the ones offered by PSTI are excellent preventive measures to reduce crime, violence and aggression in the workplace.

On-Site Training (we will come to you!)

No need to send staff away for training. PSTI will come to your place of business and train your staff.

Multiple training options for your organization:

• 2 hour Intro Courses
• 1/2 Day Training Sessions
• 1 and 2-Day Classes

AVADE® Training – www.AVADEtraining.com

A non-occupational personal safety and self-defense program which teaches YOU awareness, vigilance, avoidance, defensive interventions and escape techniques. Regardless of your occupation, AVADE® training will increase your personal safety and your ability to proactively prevent crime and violence.

SOCS® Training – www.SOCStraining.com

Security Oriented Customer Service training is a course that is designed to teach individuals how to develop habits, skills and actions for offering extraordinary customer service while maintaining safety in the workplace.

AVADE® Workplace Violence Training - www.avadetraining.com

This program is designed to increase awareness, education, prevention and mitigation of the risk of Workplace Violence in the workplace. The AVADE® training is an integral piece of an effective workplace violence plan.

**Defensive Tactics Training System –
http://personalsafetytraining.com/defensive-tactics/**

This training program covers basic defensive tactics control techniques and defensive interventions. Course includes stance, movement, escort techniques, blocking, active defense skills, handgun retention, and much more. Hundreds of Security and Law Enforcement Agencies have taken this dynamic training course.

Train-the-Trainer

(Instructor training—where we "train the trainer.") This is the most cost effective method of introducing and retaining the training programs for your agency. All of PSTI's training programs can be presented in the train-the trainer format.

OC Pepper Spray Defence -
http://personalsafetytraining.com/pepper-spray/

Tactical and Practical concepts of when and how to use pepper spray in a variety of environmental situations. Aerosol Pepper is a great non-lethal control and defense option for agencies that encounter aggressive and violent behaviors.

Handcuffing Tactics -
http://personalsafetytraining.com/handcuffing/

Security and Law-Enforcement training in the use of temporary metallic and plastic human restraints. Standing, kneeling and prone handcuffing techniques are covered. In this training course you will also learn searching, nomenclature, manufacture recommendations, drawing techniques and more.

Expandable Baton Training Techniques -
http://personalsafetytraining.com/defensive-baton/

Security and Law-Enforcement training in the use of an expandable baton, straight stick or riot control baton. Techniques and topics in this training include: vulnerable areas of the body, stance, movement, blocks, control holds, counter strikes, draws and retention techniques.

Combo-Classes
A combination of basic and instructor training where we train your staff and a select few to be trained as trainers.

Index

INDEX

INDEX

INDEX